# The Book of the Climbing Year

# The Book of the Climbing Year

CAMERON McNEISH

Patrick Stephens

**Front endpaper** *On Troutdale Pinnacle, Borrowdale, one of the classic routes in the Lake District* (Cameron McNeish).

**Rear endpaper** *The end of the route and the end of the day, at the top of Spiral Gully, Coire An t-Sneachda, Cairngorms* (Cameron McNeish).

First published in 1988


British Library Cataloguing in Publication Data

The Book of the climbing year
  1. Mountaineering
  I. McNeish, Cameron
769.5′22′0922      GV199.82

  ISBN 1-85260-043-8

Patrick Stephens Limited is part of the Thorsons Publishing Group, Wellingborough, Northamptonshire, NN8 2RQ, England.

Printed and bound in Great Britain by Butler & Tanner Ltd, Frome and London

10  9  8  7  6  5  4  3  2  1

# Contents

# Introduction

It's often been said that a climber's spirit soars and falls with the movement of the barometer. When the sun shines hot and warms the rock to the touch there is an almost insatiable desire to get to grips with that rock, to caress it, fingers searching for holds, to feel poised and in control as you swarm higher and higher.

But when it rains, depression sets in. The rock that was earlier so inviting now feigns malevolence; it looks dark and cold and wet. And yet, strangely, it is often the memory of such days that remain in the mind long after the sun-kissed glory has faded from the mind. At the end of a summer which has gone down in record as being one of the wettest ever I recall with smiling pleasure a day in mid August when an apparently easy rock climb almost took on epic proportions because it snowed. Who expects snow, or for that matter dresses for snow, in mid August? We should have realized that it can snow on any day of the year on the *North East Buttress* of Ben Nevis.

A few weeks later I climbed *Crows Nest Crack* on the North Buttress of Buachaille Etive Mor and my hands became so cold that I had to jam them in cracks one at a time while I tried to warm the other under my armpit. This was summer in the Scottish Highlands.

I make these points because we can't take the months of our year for granted. I've enjoyed glorious ski touring in October, and winter climbing in late May. I've rock climbed on sun-spoilt rock in January and hill walked in every conceivable weather in every month of the year. And that's just in Britain. No wonder climbers go to the South of France in early spring.

But one of the great attractions that climbing, in all its quirky facets, has for me is that it is an activity I can enjoy all the year round. There's no close season. The rock climbing season of spring and summer merge into the mountain padding days of late Autumn and early winter when the attraction of the Munros and big hill days strengthen me and get me fit for the long cold winter days. These are the days of big walk-ins with heavy packs to obscure snow and ice-girt crags, or long ski mountaineering trips over the high tops, days that call for a subtle level of craftsmanship and fitness. Well at least that's the theory, but as I've suggested the climbing year is subject to inherent changes depending on circumstances.

This book outlines a climbing year, each month seen through the eyes of a different climber. A lot of the action takes place in the UK, and some of it abroad in places ranging from the USA to the Himalaya. You'll read of rock climbing, snow and ice climbing, hill walking, ski touring, bouldering, Himalayan trekking and mountaineering and Alpine climbing. It's simply a celebration of the climbing year, in all its guises, in all its ambiguity, in all its controversy and in all its glory.

Cameron McNeish

# *January: Rocky Mountain High*

## GRAHAM TRUSCOTT

In the winter months the Rocky Mountains hurl their dominant mantle of ice and snow carelessly over the small towns and settlements dotted among their mighty folds and valleys. Stretching almost the length of the North American continent, from the cactus deserts of the Mexican border hundreds of miles north, through the western states of the USA and Canada to the Yukon River and the Alaskan frontier, the Rockies presented a contiguous and mighty barrier to the early settlers of the New World. In a lifetime, an individual could only make an acquaintance with a small area of their splendid immensity — and in the winter they offer the proof that they were here before the hand of man.

Perhaps if I lived amongst this variety of rock and snow I would appreciate the mountains less. As it is, I return as often as the cost of airfares

and other commitments will allow and the mountains always state their grandeur anew. In summer the 'grockles', the tourist traffickers, crowd the highways to the fringes of the National Parks — but once up on to the trails and wilderness peaks the Rockies swallow the intrusion with lofty disdain. In the winter of the Central Rockies though, the tourists cluster at the ski resorts, the downhill places to be seen, reassured by the promise of creature comforts at the end of the day and *après-ski*.

The people of the mountains, those who make the towns, those whose whole lives are here, become themselves and in the summer tourist centres strangers can be welcomed rather than merely tolerated. These people will take you into their homes at Christmas and greet you as a familiar face around town as you put together the components of your expedition. They will marvel that you should want to live in ice caves and snow shelters, miles from habitation and at altitudes far above their parish, which already has the highest YMCA camp, the highest gas station or the loftiest restaurant in the county, state or country. You must be a little odd, but they

---

*When winter snow settles on the streets of Estes Park a quiet and relaxed atmosphere pervades the town — and many others like it* (Graham Truscott).

respect you for it and offer you their homes and friendship.

My friends in these small towns are proud of their place of residence and they tell you about it. They tell you that it was founded 150 years ago, that the gold rush came and went, that a hundred years ago the 'city' did not exist. It seems incredible that the rocks which have been millenia in the making should only have known the hamburger bar and the golden arches, the pick-up truck and the 'good ol' boy' for decades. Yet here we are.

This year I am back in Estes Park, the summer tourist town that is the gateway to Rocky Mountain National Park itself — and it is gloriously out of season. The residents are in two minds about it: some are doing anything to attract business from the city of Denver ( and further afield) to keep their tourist shops open, but most have given up and closed for a long winter break. For me, however, this is the right time to be here and I have only one goal: to acclimatize, to get my act together and spend the last day of the old year and the first of the new deep in the snow coated peaks, bagging as many

as our Nordic skis will carry us to. Each December morning we meet other cross-country skiers in the Country Café for a cheap breakfast and to plan expeditions into the park. We make them, too, daily becoming more fit and adjusting to the forgotten sensations of climbing on skis and telemark turns on reckless, powdery, downhill races.

Some days we are up before dawn, motoring the ice-packed roads to the park edge and then donning skis and packs, and with muted voices moving off up into the glacial landscape above the town. This is the easy way of doing things — each night we have warm showers and bunks available — but by day we are on our own. The scene is ours but for the occasional rare trail of another skier, or, more commonly that of a coyote, ptarmigan or crow.

Back at the Country Café there is news of a National Outdoor Leadership School expedition to the north over the period that we want to climb. Some of us thought of the Teton Range in Wyoming, and this will take place in the Wind River's — practically next door and south-east of Yellowstone. In the end, though, it's only me

*The frozen logging road is our starting point as gear is unloaded from the four-wheel drive trucks* (Graham Truscott).

*Snow kitchen and tarp over sleeping bags on the dawn of the New Year* (Graham Truscott).

who wants to join the NOLS group. Phil drives the icy roads north in our $300 Mercury monster to take me there, before, like my other Colorado friends, moving on to other places and his own adventures. Suddenly, I am part of the Wind River Expedition, meeting new ski mountaineers and after days in the car and some rough nights, I'm swinging back into training again.

It is more serious now, I am part of a team, trying to fit in with other strangers, determined, like them, to weld together a success; determined to spend the deepest winter month relying on our own resources, on what we can carry on our backs-in isolated splendour — in the mountains.

By 31 December we are well into the Wind River Range, having been dropped off by four-wheel drive some miles from a logging camp

two days before. It is an unusual experience to be climbing with people that I have only known for a matter of days, but there is nothing like sharing the camp chores and the same igloo with someone to come to know them quickly. It is an interesting team: three NOLS instructors; two military men, one a Marine; four women, two of whom are physical education instructors; and myself, like one of the girls, a refugee from city life hundreds of miles away. On these first few days as we move into the Wind River Range and up towards the Continental Divide (the watershed which determines whether the Atlantic or Pacific oceans will benefit from precipitation falling on this land) we begin to see each other's strengths and weaknesses, even decide whether we like each other or not. I am always surprised how often one determines such things very early on in a relationship, but here there has to be a commitment to get on and work together — the group depends on its parts, wherever they come from, whatever they can do.

The likelihood is that once we come down from the mountains we will separate and go our different ways but it is hard to see that far ahead when there are the pressing camp chores to organize each day. By New Year's Eve there has already been some definition of roles and responsibilities as tasks become shared out on the basis of ability rather than equality. It makes sense, if only to spare us all from fried 'mush' with too much curry powder — for breakfast! Nobody believes that I mistook the curry for dried egg powder, but it doesn't look as if I will be doing much cooking.

The irony is that by this end of the old year and beginning of the new we are surprisingly well-settled into the rhythm of a very basic existence and expedition life. I find myself 'volunteered' to get the Primus stove going to bring the others the necessary first round of morning hot drinks. We try to drink about three pints a day each, preferably more, to avoid dehydration through a strenuous day's uphill skiing. Morning rituals evolve, from the first hot drinks to the washing up (a scouring of saucepans with snow) and the preparation of hot water bottles for each person's pack for the day. Melting snow for this task keeps the primus stoves busy until they are the last items to be packed.

Our New Year's Eve camp, by the edge of a belt of pine and spruce trees, is an easy one to construct as we are able to burrow into the drifts against the trees. After supper we gather to see out the old and ring in the new a good five or six hours early, trusting to time and the men with their fingers on the nuclear buttons across the world that it will happen. We dance briefly, layered four, five or six items deep against the cold, around our snow kitchens, arm in arm like old friends, before crawling back into shelters and Arctic sleeping bags, to tell tall stories, until we fall asleep.

The new year dawns clearer than any day yet, making a brilliant change from the snowstorm conditions prevailing when we left the logging camp road. For the first New Year's Day for many a year for some of us we wake clearheaded and eager to be on the move. Cold, intense enough to freeze bare skin to metal, silent enough to shout at the immensity of uniform blue sky above, sparkles over pristine fresh snow. We are keen to make the most of what looks like the beginning of a good period of settled weather. In these conditions, navigation could hardly be easier — the shapes of the peaks above, beyond and around us are as distinctive as one could wish as we climb the ridge opposite last year's camp and stride over into the next and higher valley.

The tracks of coyote criss-cross a small frozen lake and as we move up through the scrub trees we see the shambling tracks of porcupine and lighter prints from hardy birds that winter on these slopes. It is tough work pushing uphill, conversation is infrequent and sometimes earthy. We take it in turns to break trail — the stronger members of the team giving it longer than those who tire more quickly.

At one point we're startled by fresh blood, vivid red against the white and darker trees: the scattered remnants of a snow hare hastily dropped by a cautious coyote, probably disturbed by our intrusive approach across the valley floor. The consumer of this interrupted feast is long gone and not one of us catches so much as a glimpse of the raider. Again unseen by us, he will return when we have safely passed by. Meals such as this cannot come easily in the depth of winter and it will not be abandoned to the stoat or ermine.

In the scrub trees the going becomes increasingly difficult. We change trail breakers more frequently, rest more often, concentrate on our footwork and stop to pick each other up several times. After a while we even stop grading our clumsy falls. It takes a lot of energy to recover from a fall since it usually involves

unbuckling one's pack and, once upright again, lifting it back into position. We lunch on the move: traditional trail mix, heavily biased towards nuts rich in protein and fats. Air temperatures remain tens of degrees below freezing, but dazzling sun (we are all wearing glacier goggles now) and the warmth of our exertions soon have us adjusting the clothing mix.

As we climb, the slope becomes steeper yet. We cope by tightening our zigzagging turns until we are forced to line skis with skins for greater adhesion. By 2.30 pm, (not that clocks have much meaning here) we have gained the top of the ridge and begun to edge our way northwards along it, gradually sliding our way over into the next river catchment.

It is towards dusk the following day that it becomes clear that one of our party is having trouble. Jayne's complaints about headaches and tiredness are matched by a subtle slowing of her movements and increasing tendency to lag behind. Since we know that she has come up very quickly from the coast near Cape Cod only five days before it seems possible that the problem could be altitude sickness and as the symptoms persist and worsen, the necessity to get her down to a lower elevation and out of the mountains develops with frightening rapidity. The night's shelters are already built and supper is ready: there is little we can do this evening, but the decision is made to detach a team of three to escort Jayne as rapidly as possible back to the logging road the following morning, carrying the contents of her pack between them. From there we will attempt to find a logging truck and secure her a ride back to the nearest settlement some fifty miles away on the edge of the Wind River Indian Reservation back out in the foothills of these mountains. Jayne begins to feel the cold more — or rather we feel it for her, plying her with hot liquids and warming her feet against our stomachs in the shelter of this evening's snow cave.

The night is unusually restless. Until now we have all slept well after our daily exertions, but Jayne constantly disturbs the other girl to whom she's zipped her sleeping bag for warmth and the two wake the other half of the shelter more than once. For some reason — physiologists may have an explanation — each person wakened discovers the need to empty his or her bladder. There's a succession of curses as each of us has to leave the comfort of the sleeping bag and don layers of clothing scattered within each cocoon of Hollofil or duck down to brave the brief trek outside.

The morning comes and, after a hurried breakfast, we four, Jayne with an all-but-empty pack, begin to retrace our tracks of the previous days. We make sure that Jayne is escorted closely, but we enjoy skiing quickly back downslope then waiting for her to catch up. We return to our second night's camp in one day and it is noticeable how different this former camp feels to be occupied by only four, one of whom is sick. Using only one of the three shelters that we had built reinforces the emptiness, although our colleagues are on the slopes behind and beyond us, and hardly gone for ever.

In another day we have arrived back at the logging road, pleased with the time that we have made and reassured that Jayne seems if not better, then at least no worse: the altitude sickness will pass as we descend. Three of us build a 'quincy' (an old Indian word for a snow shelter constructed by piling snow in a heap and then burrowing into it) within sight of the road, but before we have finished we hear a convoy of trucks negotiating the ice-packed track and rush out to stop them for assistance. Rob, one of our leaders, and Jayne cadge a ride, leaving just two as the night settles in around us, and the taillights and growling engines recede below.

If the stark, silent intensity of the day has impressed us, the enormity of night overwhelms the more so. The sky is so huge, dark space so close, stars so many, so near and unreachable that we are glad to burrow down to escape the implications for our relevance to it all, utterly awed. It is an experience we savour every clear evening — and most are completely cloudless — of our month in the wilderness, but this night, as we wonder about Jayne and are not distracted by our fellow ski-mountaineers, infinity is more immediate than ever. The winter night skies of the high Rockies are one of the wonders of the universe.

By late the following afternoon Rob has returned to us, delivered by a NOLS snowmobile which departs as soon as it has dropped him off. He is tired by the long journey with Jayne and back, but reports that all is well and that she will recover in time. Once again I thank my period of acclimatization in Colorado prior to joining this group, but then we're deep into plans to rejoin the others some 15 miles away and nearly 3,000 ft higher than we are now. There is some serious skiing to be done, but we plot a route

along and up the first valley along the Continental Divide and up to our anticipated rendezvous point at 10,000 ft.

As we approach our colleagues' camp the next afternoon we pick out specks skiing down a broad bowl from a small peak above. We realize that they are on their way down having 'bagged' the summit above them earlier in the day, probably after a very early start. As the two parties get closer to each other and approach the camp, they wave their success and we the rescue team, retreat into self-righteousness in defence and envy.

Encouraged and now confident that we have a fit team after over a week on skis, we depart the next morning a reunited band of alpine explorers *en route* to the challenge of Union Peak. Even in Wyoming there must be dozens of summits with this ubiquitous American name, but we have our thoughts set on one of just over 12,000 ft and not too far away. It is in our view all day as we cross a variety of snow conditions, from deep drifts against imposing outcrops to frozen lakes with patches of pure ice, blue and polar. Several times we stop to rewax skis, but find it difficult to get the balance quite right and eventually most of us settle for a softer application and leave it at that.

Camp is at about 10,000 ft but it is later than usual before construction begins. Supper is prepared as we work in shifts on igloo and quincy building. We make the snow shelters on the small side and this brings problems as, tired and anxious to complete our task, I am burrowing into a pile of snow with Ros. Ros digs with frantic energy. I suggest that we pace ourselves, and warn her that as dusk falls outside we can no longer rely upon light shining through our snow roof to indicate when the dome overhead is becoming too frail to support itself. We dig to the depth of the ski poles stuck through the sides instead. Suddenly, there is a dull 'crump' and I'm swallowing snow, pushing my way upwards to where I know that there must be air. I reach down beside me and drag out Ros, as our fellow shelter dwellers turn from their tasks by the stove to stare at us — and the roofless quincy — in disbelief.

There is little time for recriminations. Night has fallen, the air temperature is $-40°C$ and tired people need shelter fast. After earnest discussion we decide to rig a tarpaulin over the remains of the quincy walls, but warm drinks fail to disguise the absence of an insulating 2 ft layer of snow above us. Shedding even fewer layers of

**Above** *Camp on the western side of the frozen lake. The quincy on the right has been repaired after an uncomfortable night without a 2 ft insulating layer of snow above our heads* (Graham Truscott).

clothing than usual, we decide on four sleeping bags between five of us to further minimize heat loss.

It is a fitful night. Normally we can raise the temperature within a shelter to just about freezing point: raised platforms within and entrances below floor level keep out draughts and retain warmth. Tonight there are no tall stories. As Jayne's departure has already taught us, bad situations blow up out of nowhere and can become serious in no time at all. If the stove failed, had one of use been hurt we would be in trouble, for in the other two shelters, also built small tonight, there is no spare room, or heat, and only two other stoves.

The morning brings cloud and a welcome rise in temperatures as a blizzard sets in. We construct a new pile of snow and this time

**Right** *After a cold night in a collapsed snow shelter, the task of rebuilding begins* (Graham Truscott).

*Sleeping bags air in the morning's sun while we practise telemark turns and skiing technique on the slope beyond the igloo at one of our lower camps* (Graham Truscott).

burrow successfully. We shelter and sleep for 36 hours fast against the storm. From the mouth of our shelter the other two are visible — but only just. Periodic excursions light stoves and prepare hot drinks and calorie-rich foods, clearing each time the white overburden which has hidden packs and fuel bottles. Jez goes out at one point for a private moment to commune with nature and returns puffing and flustered, convinced that a coyote, intent on using the same rock for much the same purpose is out to dispute the territory. We are willing to believe that if there was a coyote, it was more scared of Jez, and Jez's denials receive a raucous laughter, which says much for our team spirit and willingness to get back underway.

Camp is on the slopes of Union Peak. We are by a small frozen lake or tarn whose exact dimensions it is impossible to determine against the blanket whiteness of the landscape. But there's no hope of fishing, for we cannot break through the ice to the water below (if there is any) — even with ice saws — it must be more than 3 ft thick. Poor fish — or are they lucky not to be caught and roasted by us?

Finally, one evening, the storm clears, rising to give us a miraculous sunset, reflected on the snow as vididly as in the sky above. We are awestruck at the edge of the lake, but cameras cannot capture the moment and we will find later that we have only caught the tail-end of the spectacle above us from our grandstand seats near the trees by the snow kitchens, packs and shelters.

Brilliant dawn and clear views of the Tetons to the West inspire us to tackle Union Peak behind us, and we gather kit for the attempt. We plan to go up and return to this camp in a day. Avalanche transponders are checked, sleeping bags, stove and extra provisions carried in case of accident, and the steady climb begins. It is steady, a slightly faster pace than is really comfortable and relentless. There is little talking and much will-power; steep, tight turns and gradients at the limits of our skis. Camp is soon very far away and we are well above the tree-line. There is nothing particularly glorious about a mid-winter assault on an insignificant peak like this beyond our own enjoyment of the challenge and it is our own satisfaction that will count. We are not playing at climbing — we are here doing it for real at least two or three days from outside help if we get into trouble. We are going to do this *on skis* — we're determined.

Uphill we plough in shortening zigzags until we hit rock and ice too steep, too hard to offer purchase. Skis are shed and crampons donned with grunts of annoyance as they are tightened to fit and straps fastened with clumsy gloved fingers. We take poles and an ice axe each too, but the latter are hardly needed: the wind — it must be 50 mph up here — helps the climb. Turn back into it, even for a moment and bitter slivers of ice cut into what little skin remains exposed on the face and penetrate layers of insulation with dangerous chill. For a while, we are rock climbing, but hide the 'feel' of the rock. Then I look up from all fours to find Jez grinning at me from a small plateau which leads to the summit cairn and marker. Within a few minutes we are all there, trying to take celebratory photographs without being blown clean off the other side of the peak, for there is no way to escape the force of that wind bowling over the top. On the descent we caution ourselves, especially after starting a small avalanche by accidentally disturbing a cornice on a ridge to the right of our upward scramble. But the ridge seems to offer a slightly easier way back to the point at which we abandoned skis and we follow it down.

Once skis are reclaimed and ice axes stowed again. It is a beautiful, long, smooth, powdery glissade through the bowl of the mountain, turning in wide sweeping telemarks, carving furrowed tracks against the massive slope behind. Quarter of a mile apart we are specks on the surface of the universe and it feels fantastic! The knowledge of our location and self-reliance does somewhat temper our reckless desire to chase and turn downhill at speed in sheer exhilaration, but it is an excited group which assembles at the base of the bowl to ski the flatter portions of the route back to camp across the lake at sunset.

The next morning this camp has served its purpose and it is abandoned as we move on towards the next objective, a peak we have finally decided upon in the flush of yesterday's success: five miles away as the crow flies, but rather further by our more laborious movement and heavy packs. After the lighter packs carried on yesterday's climb, today's seem doubly heavy. There are few incidents to relieve the 'march' and the evening's camp is chosen with little discussion and built with routine efficiency, but then comes disappointment. Clouds gather

overnight and we are into another two-day or possibly three-day storm which, allowing another day to reach and two to climb the next mountain, will not leave time to get back to our rendezvous point for the conclusion of the expedition.

Holed up by the weather we practise some compass work near the camp and there is plenty of opportunity to talk through our options — the number of which decreases as the weather worsens. Finally, still in poor visibility and settling snow, we accept that time is against us and depart north-westwards, reluctantly subduing the ambition to tackle a further summit. There is nearly a week of steady movement between river basins, however, back over the Continental Divide, and much of the pleasure of being here is still to be enjoyed. We take some pride in using our compasses accurately on this first morning of the return journey and, once underway, treat this journey as a new ski-mountaineering challenge in which to improve techniques and abilities. As we have done throughout, we take turns to break trail and it is curious how our skills at reading the snow, the angle of slope and picking the best tactical route over each few hundred yards to our destination for the day have improved. We move with much greater efficiency of effort, even on steep up-slopes, with fewer falls.

One of the new experiences of this journey back towards a more complicated world are some closer encounters (if you except Jez's coyote!) with wildlife. One morning we find ermine tracks along the shelves of our snow kitchen carved out the night before. The animal has succeeded in breaking into a polythene bag of food — a bag of trail mix and there is great debate about whether the stoat family actually eats nuts, coconut and dried fruit! Disbelievers even suggest that the bag had been broken anyway, should not have been left out overnight and that the tracks suggest our visitor was more interested in scraps from the cleaned out cooking utensils anyway. It is a good topic of conversation until camp is packed and we spread out long a valley side, descending through trees on a brilliant cold blue day.

Near the tree–line, on the limits of conditions under which the ubiquitous varieties of native firs will grow, knarled and twisted remnants of trees long dead, weathered by successive winters and baked by summer suns point their sculptured, tortured limbs to the heavens and along our route. On many, the bark has gone

*The author standing by the summit marker on Union Peak, back turned to the wind* (Graham Truscott Collection).

and the wood is worn smooth by wind, ice and elemental forces of the natural world around us. These poor dead boughs are things of beauty, but to rest and admire for too long, even to pause for a snack or to take in the wider views to mountains 20, 30, or even 40 miles away is to invite the air and wind to rob the heat you have generated on the move. Energy conservation, putting on additional layers before cold strikes, has become second nature.

Three nights from our collection point we are treated to a prehistoric chorus, which has us glad of our snug shelters and human company. After supper, as we enter our caves of snow an eerie howl is carried across the valley before us. It is joined by another, closer by and then there are others up and down the slopes and from both the left and right of our position. Those of us who have not yet entered the quincy, sense a primitive rising of the hair on our necks and

terrible shivers down the spine. The full moon — just like in the story books — lights the snow. We think we see low shapes flitting along the edge of the trees opposite, perhaps half a mile away — it could be imagination. The coyotes continue to call each other for some 30 minutes as we try to move silently to catch a glimpse of them. Eventually, the cold begins to grope through our quilted jackets, overtrousers and many layers and we turn to the comfort of sleeping bags within.

The next night, lower still and camping among tress we try to blend more with our environment, making as little sound as possible as we establish our rest stop for the night. Reward comes as we are eating our meal in the gathering dusk, a sensation rather than a sound, an awareness more than a sighting of heavy animals moving through the woods around us, once again on both sides of the camp. Elk, a sizeable herd all around us in the darkness, like us using the firs for shelter, like us moving on, moving downhill towards less barren landscapes. Where the previous evening's experience was mystical, tonight's is almost magical. We cannot believe our luck as they pass by. We are spellbound for 15 minutes until they are gone about their way and the incipient loss of feeling in our toes and faces reminds us of our first priority to stay warm. I am reminded too of a similar moment some weeks before, back in Colorado. In Estes Park late one evening staggering through a deserted town with friends we were astonished by elk crossing the main street ahead of us, moving through a blanketing snow storm to lower elevations and utterly ignoring the buildings, parked vehicles and lights of man. Tonight we are in their environment and deeply respectful of it.

We reach our destination early and camp some two or three hours away from the pre-arranged meeting point, planning to ski down in style and at some speed the following morning, perhaps having dropped our packs off there first, but such ideas are quickly dispelled as Chris, attempting to twist a fast independent path to the valley floor from a point just below the camp, catches an edge on a fallen tree barely visible beneath a diguise of snow and fetches his right knee a vicious crack against the frozen log. For a moment, he is too winded to cry out and then he is in tremendous pain. We all ski towards him at once and then, realizing that the injury is serious, swing into a rehearsed emergency routine. A sleeping bag is fetched, a stove brought out and lit, water boiled for hot drinks and warm bottles placed beside the casualty, under his outer layer of clothes. Unable to move, and shocked, Chris is rapidly getting cold. We despatch a team to the meeting point, to ski towards the snowmobiles that are due to pick us up to direct them immediately to Chris's assistance. The rest of us do what we can to make him comfortable where he has fallen, raiding the first aid kit for pain relief but reluctant to give him anything too strong as long as he appears to be able to cope with the hurt in true military tradition. Fortunately qualified medical attention is available within a few hours, for the first time in four weeks.

The snowmobiles are late, but eventually their noisy intrusive roar is heard approaching up the valley. We have fashioned a temporary splint for the injured leg and Chris is lifted gingerly on to a sled, before being wrapped once more in sleeping bags and towed away with two people hanging on to the sled sides to hold him steady. Those left behind load their packs aboard another sled and we ski a last exhilarating few miles unencumbered to the point on the logging road where the four-wheel drive vehicles await us. While we have been away logging operations have been suspended and the road is no longer trodden down by the trucks: this is the furthest point that our vehicles have been able to reach.

By the time we arrive at the pick-up trucks Chris has already been transferred and driven away. We do not catch up with him again for another 12 hours, a weary journey down the winding logging road and by road back to Lander. By a large open fire in the great hallway of the former hotel that is NOLS headquarters today he's resting: his kneecap has been shattered by the fall and will eventually require surgery to repair. In the meantime the hospital has cleaned him up and he is surprisingly philosophical about this abrupt and unexpected end to a month's serious skiing and climbing. Rob, the instructor, even makes him feel fortunate by citing comparisons with others in his experience who have come to grief in skiing accidents, including one whose attempts to jump a cornice and 'do some airtime' resulted in a fall on to the point of his ski and the permanent loss of one eye. The gruesome measures required to summon medical assistance for that injury, some days from outside help hardly bear thinking about.

In the main though, we are pleased with all that we have seen and done, the distance we

**Far left** *The descent from Union Peak gives an impression of the vastness of the landscape in which we are living: Tetons, again, on the skyline* (Graham Truscott).

**Below left** *This is as far as skis will carry us on Union Peak: beyond this it is a few hours' scrambling with crampons and ice axes to the smooth summit* (Graham Truscott).

**Left** *One evening in particular, the sky is so spectacular that we can only watch by the snow kitchens, warm drinks in hand, and admire* (Graham Truscott).

have travelled, the two peaks some of us have climbed, and one that we all (bar Jayne) ascended. We are pleased, that is, until an informal debriefing session over dinner and then a more formal one later the following day after an unaccustomed night in normal beds (albeit ancient ones). We analyse our reactions to each other, to the two casualties, to living in the snow, and assess how well we really welded together as a team. A curious difference in view emerges: the girls all feel, to varying degrees, that the men, Jez and I in particular, tended to be too brash and impetuous. It is a criticism that we feel

is unfounded, though impetuous skiing, we concede, may have contributed to Chris's accident. Does it really warrant such soul-searching inquiry? Jez and I decide that, this time, it does not, and we go out to climb a three-story icefall around a drainpipe at the back of the hostel in the gathering dusk.

It takes time for all the implications of a prolonged period of climbing like this to sink in. A thousand little incidents on the trail, on the rock and ice climbs and descents are soon forgotten by the conscious mind, but knowledge of techniques, means of working with others and

*Moving the injured party the easy way. Chris is fortunate that his accident occurred within comparatively easy reach of assistance* (Graham Truscott).

native skills have been sharpened. The legacies of those events — and the memories — come back in new situations, with other people, on different hills and climbs in months and years to come.

Our time in the Rockies is not as divorced in the memory as it seemed then from other events in our lives, but I have other places to seek out and activities to pursue. I am not quite irresponsible enough to live only for skiing and climbing — not now, but I will return to the Rockies — and in winter too — and I will live among them, climb freely, and ski again, as I did this one month, this year, this January.

Regarding the 'outdoor experience' as a vital part of life's rich tapestry, Graham Truscott, a former researcher with the *National Geographic* magazine in Washington DC, a fellow of the Royal Geographic Society and a committed conservationist has hiked, skied and climbed in many parts of Britain and North America. Working now in the United Kingdom, he is also a keen inland and coastal sailor and canoeist.

# *February: A Scottish Winter Climb*

## KEN CROCKET

### Moon

A cynic would remark that with only 28 days to its name, February is soon over, and good riddance, too. It can be a cruel and fickle month, February can, though from a climber's stance I have always found it to be more true than January, if less friendly than March. Asked to sum up the three true winter months with one word each, then gales, cold, and sun would be as good a three as any, fitting the months of January, February and March. So to the cold one, February, known to the early tillers as the 'fill-dike' month, for its propensity to fill ditches with snow, water, dead livestock and anything else.

> February, fill the dyke,
> With what thou dost like.
>
> (Thomas Tusser:
> (*Five Hundred Points of Good Husbandry*)

Unfortunately, in Scotland a dike (or more usually dyke) is a wall, and not a ditch, but we can still see the snow pile up against the drystane dykes in a good February blizzard, so the poetic imagery can remain. So what, from a score of averagely mediocre climbing Februaries, can I offer up as potentially interesting experiences?

Beginning weekending in the late 1960s, I was, like most of my contemporaries, under the spell of W H Murray's classic books. To my unformed and easily-moulded psyche some of his best passages were of moonlight expeditions, and so I lay in wait for the right night, and the right victim to share it with. The chance came up in February 1968. The Glasgow University Mountaineering Club, then suffering me as a gauche if enthusiastic novice, was staying at Steall Hut, Glen Nevis. This is a climbers' hut in a beautiful and even romantic setting, embedded like an uncut gem at the start of the upper section of the Glen and reached by a Himalayan-type path through an impressive gorge, white water crashing hundreds of feet below, a step away from

disaster. I made the approach with a small plastic torch firmly planted in my ample mouth. A nervous gulp at the wrong moment and medical history would have been made, lights dimming in lecture theatres all over Europe for the presentation of 'The Illuminated Man'.

The gauntlet of the gorge was successfully run, however, to come up against the other defences of the hut. This was a wire bridge of dubious engineering, negotiated with some fear after an evening at some Fort William drinking den, one's natural tendency to sway amplified by its freely suspended catenary. Had I but thought then, romance might have entered my life earlier, helping some maiden across the rushing waters, but I suffered from tunnel vision and climbing was all. On the Saturday of the meet, my ears pricked up in the pub when two older members announced a moonlight expedition. I determined to follow suit, and turned my powers of persuasion on an unsuspecting fellow member. Les his name was. It was after the pub had closed, and though Les was a stolid non-drinker, he needed no persuasion to go out again into that brilliant moonlight night. I had to persuade him of my sobriety. Shortly afterwards, my pathetic collection of equipment was together and off up the Glen we set.

The river under the wire bridge twinkled hypnotically under the moon, so that we were glad to reach the creaking snow on the far bank. I, in my youthful enthusiasm, had thought of walking up a peak that same night, but Les, whose natural caution would probably always doom him to a safe if dull course through life, decreed a walk to the head of the Glen, some four miles, with a bivouac there. This would be followed the next morning with a hill or two, if I were still alive that is. Half an hour out of the hut, having crashed down several times on an ice-sheeted path, I wore crampons for the first time. A word here about the crampons. My native city, Glasgow, then had no climbing shop, despite having an

*Late afternoon, looking west from Aonach Beag over Glen Nevis to the Mamores* (Ken Crocket).

embarrassing concentration of good climbers, and my crampons had been found being remaindered in a local sports shop, the only pair, sitting in the huff between the fishing rods and the skipping ropes. The fit was awful, rattling on my boots, and they had no front points, but they cost only £3 or so and had to do. At home I wedged an old door against a wall and stomped up and down like an aged guide instructing a new pupil. It didn't do much for the door, but it worried the family and puzzled the dog.

On the Glen Nevis path that brilliant night, the crampons had little demanded of them. Just as well, since their straps appeared to consist of coconut fibre, with no obvious inherent strength. We walked on winding, glittering ribbons of water ice, an imposter moon mirrored at our feet. Going east along the empty glen, the real moon sailed above the Mamore Hills to our right, icy peaks a terrible height above. There was nothing warm and soft about these hills tonight, despite their etymology. The path lay on a slope running down to the Water of Nevis on the right, the river mostly hidden in the shadow of the mountains. Shadows, one soon discovers in moonlight, are very dark indeed, with a landscape familiar in the daylight transmuted into something strange and wonderful by the weak, reflected light of the moon. The Steall Waterfall, soon left behind, was partly frozen, water tinkling treacherously behind its alter ego, a glittering, if imperfect column.

My delight at the colours expressed by the ice crystals in the snow was complete. The full moon in February soars above all others, dimming even Orion's Belt. With eyes fully adapted to the dark, the rich spectrum of colours internally reflected from minute crystals of ice could be savoured; sapphire blues, darker than any sky, pulsing reds seen nowhere else in nature, and perhaps best of all the mysterious range of purples, richer than any emperor's cloak. Within one crystal, formed perhaps miles high in the atmosphere, lying indistinguishable from its countless neighbours and soon to be taken back to the atmosphere, lay a world that gave me much pleasure.

After walking for a few hours we reached a small hillock called Tom an Eite, just short of

**Above**  *Looking east from Aonach Beag, over Glen Nevis to the Mamores* (Ken Crocket).

**Below**  *The view south from Aonach Beag over Glen Nevis to the Mamores* (Ken Crocket).

the watershed. It also marked the birthplace of the Water of Nevis, which made an abrupt left turn at this point, growing suddenly in stature from a small burn out of the coire between Sgurr Eilde Mor and Binnein Mor. Incongruously parked at this point, our chosen halt for what was left of the night, was a tractor. It might have been a spaceship, given that there was no road for miles. What it was doing there and how it had arrived remains a mystery. There was also a small, aluminium workman's hut, firmly padlocked against needy souls such as we two. My companion Les opened out his down sleeping bag and prepared his spot on the snow. I had a summer 'snuff-it' bag of thin nylon, whose two doubtful features were those of cheapness and the little built-in pillow. There was no shelter save the tractor, under whose diesel aroma I wriggled my cocoon. Luckily there was no real wind, only a light movement of cold air, more sensed than felt, while the stars shone the harder as the moon sank behind the mountains. For the first time I felt the size of these mountains, their massive, passive bulk, their age beyond mere human understanding. I dozed and woke up through the night, and the mountains travelled through the stars, with me safely in their fold.

The next time I woke to hear Les exclaiming at the sight. It was dawn, and directly north of us the summits of the Grey Coires were glowing pink with the first rays of the sun. The colour was gone in minutes, fading perceptibly before the brighter light of day. I moved stiffly to the burn for water, which froze in the dixie before I had walked more than 30 feet back to the stove Les had lit. Immediately behind us was the most remote summit of the Mamores, Sgurr Eilde Mor, 'the big peak of the hind'. After a minimal breakfast we ploughed up deep snow to its summit, but I, a teenager with stamina as yet untrained, baulked at the next peak. This was Binnein Mor, the biggest of the Mamores, and I had had enough. We returned to the hut via the Glen, memories saturated with the colours and sights from a moonlight walk in February.

## Cold

Next year saw the University Club taking their February mid-term meet up to Loch Laggan, between Spean Bridge and Newtonmore. No luxury hut this time, the bulk of the

participants slumming it in disused and falling-down chalets behind the Laggan Inn. I got off relatively lightly, as I was in a tent. We had the mixed blessing of perfect weather, so that each brilliant, sunny day was followed by exceptionally low temperatures throughout the long, cold nights. At nearby Newtonmore, we later heard, the official low for the weekend was -2°F, that is, 34°F below freezing. We stayed in the grip of frost from when the sun dipped in the mid-afternoon until late the next morning, stumbling about, puffing out short-lived balloons of water vapour in the air. One club member woke up, reached the door of the chalet, and promptly collapsed. He blamed it on fumes from a cooking stove, but he may well have been the victim of mild hypothermia.

We were unused to such low temperatures, and were mostly ill-equipped to handle it. Routine events such as cooking caused much amusement. Eggs froze so hard that they could be thrown with force against a wall, only to bounce off, unbroken. They had to be boiled before they could be fried. One unexpected bonus was the transformation of tinned custard into a rare and delectable ice cream.

After the first morning, struggling to jam feet into rock-hard leather boots, I learned to take the boots into the sleeping bag for a half-hour's thawing session, hugging the lumpen objects and kneading them until their ankles softened. Loch Laggan also complained volubly about the cold. It was frozen over, an eye-blinding white expanse. During the day, when the sun hit the surface, the expansions and contractions of such a huge area of ice led to an impressive barrage of noises - *Sinfonia Antartica*. Immense, irregular cracks appeared, a giant's crazy paving. These were accompanied by basso rumblings, tortured screeches and sharper reports in counterpoint. It was so frightening and obviously unstable that we dared not venture closer, despite our fascination.

The idea was to climb on nearby Creag Meaghaidh. A bold band of us walked in on the first morning but soon found the deep powder snow and hard water ice unaccommodating. As yet, most of us students could not afford a pair of gaiters, so that the inevitable cuff of ice formed round each ankle, formed by the refreezing of snow melted by warmer socks above. I did have a padded jacket, designed, I imagine, for standing about on football terraces, and stuffed with cotton. This worked as long as it remained dry. The technology of climbing was, however, beginning to creep in to my awareness, and I had acquired a plastic safety helmet from a friend, who knew a friend, who worked on a building site. With its front brim sawn off, this garish yellow covering imbued a false sense of security. I had recently bought an ice axe from Black's of Greenock. I have it still, and cannot understand how I had the strength to hold it above my head for more than 20 minutes, let alone cut steps with it. It was too long for climbing, and I was to have it shortened twice during my few years of cutting steps.

On Creag Meaghaidh that day I cut my first steps on a route, passing some time on the first 20 feet of 1959 Face Route, now a classic Grade IV first recorded by the Olympean team of Marshall, Stenhouse and Haston. At the rate we progressed up the first ice step, we estimated that 20 hours might see the top, and we retreated much depressed.

There was no real respite in the inn at nights, where a miserable fire struggled ineffectively against the mightier cold outside. The beer was just off freezing and agony to drink, while the water supply had frozen long ago, but we howled out our collection of folk songs, accompanied by some good guitar playing, before steeling ourselves to breathe the Siberian air.

The second day was much more fun. We went to Creagh Dubh, that infamously steep roadside crag just south of Newtonmore. Amazingly enough, in the still air and relatively warm sun it was possible to rock climb on the lower tier of rock. We climbed a Severe called Mirador, easy enough in stiff boots with accommodating, flat holds. Then my partner Dave and myself were transfixed by a shout for help over on the left, where one of the club, not renowned for thinking things through, had run into some trouble on a steep Very Severe. Some 60 feet up, with no runners, a large flake had broken off. More by instinct than anything else, he had managed to grab another hold and there he clung, gibbering. We scurried up the remainder of our climb, traversed over above him, and lowered the end of our rope to his grateful clutches.

More prolonged fun was provided by Fred, the vegetative gully at the right of the main wall. The upper part of Creagh Dubh was sheathed in ice, mostly icicles draped over the

steep walls and roofs which make climbing here so exciting. In the warm sun these would loosen and crash down, many being funnelled into good old Fred's gullet. Like 'Old Faithful', the geyser in Yellowstone Park which erupts on schedule, Fred would announce the next avalanche with a low, far-off rumble. The crashing would rise in pitch, and finally the gully would disdainfully eject a bizarre mix of ice and rocks, scattering us students. More dangerous were the 'erratics', rocks and lumps of ice which would come hurtling down over the cliff with little warning. The final straw came when a far-off whistling sound announced a real flyer. Looking up, a black object seemed to be growing in size incredibly quickly. Instinct prompted a forward somersault on to the scree slope in front, and the boulder missed. It also missed, by a few feet, a tiny French girl, sitting through all the excitement with a commendable Gallic calm, improving the suntan. After that we persuaded her to move to a safer location.

At last the long weekend drew to a halt. The minibus drove south and disgorged its passengers on the north side of town. Penniless by now, I still had to reach home on the wrong side of town. Economies had dictated no change of footwear, so wearing stiff leather boots, with rucksack and holdall, I trudged the midnight miles down through the quiet city. The stars were as jaded as my spirits when I limped in through the door, both feet bleeding profusely. Nowadays of course, my plastic friend would open a cash dispenser, I would hire a taxi and cruise home. But I was still earning my stripes, I was becoming a climber.

## Wind

The next weekend, heels still in plasters, I made what was to be one of several attempts to climb the Upper Couloir of Stob Ghabhar. This is a classic Grade II with a long approach walk, in effect a spiral ascent of this very fine mountain to the west of Loch Tulla, near Bridge of Orchy. For various reasons, and despite my slowly increasing competence, this short and easy route defied all my efforts for many years. The cold spell from the previous weekend was still holding as we approached the route, a narrow gully splitting the very summit rocks of the hill. The cold was intense, made worse by a bitter wind. At the foot of the gully, I realized that the side of my face exposed to the wind had become completely numb. It was like tapping a slab of wood, an effect akin to an injection at the dentist, but without any mobility of the skin. It was too miserable to put crampons on, and after poking ineffectually at the ice pitch for ten minutes we retreated, traversing right under the face to find an easier way up.

> '..such a February face, so full of frost, of storm and cloudiness'.
> (*Much Ado About Nothing,* Act V)

On the summit we put our crampons on, as there were icy patches and descent had to be safeguarded. Going down the south ridge of Stob Ghabhar we experienced what felt like a local jetstream, with a continual and extremely strong wind howling over us from the east. My recently-acquired yellow workman's helmet, held on by a chinstrap, was ripped off and flew towards the Atlantic, not even stopping to bounce. We reeled about, held only by our crampon points, as streaks of mist rushed by. The wind ripping over my anorak pockets

produced a vacuum effect, and a compass was sucked out. It fell on the snow and I pounced on it before it joined the helmet. It was time to go, view or no view.

As we descended the hill towards the glen the wind dropped and we were able to appreciate the colours in the snow, deep blues appearing in every cavity, something to do with the crystal structure we supposed, and uncommon at this intensity. We cared little for crystal structure at this point, being grateful to be in one piece. It had been a hard month, and I was yet to make a winter ascent.

## Climbing

By 1972 I was climbing at Hard VS and Grade IV, though the elusive Grade V was yet to happen, as was the Upper Couloir of Stob Ghabhar. We were still cutting steps, barely aware of experiments being performed by various climbers in different countries, experiments which would completely change winter climbing and which would eventually eliminate the century-old technique of hacking out steps with a single axe. To illustrate the

*The winter cliffs of Stob Coire nan Lochan (Peak of the Coire of the Lochan), with the South, Central and North Buttresses. The gully just above the shadow is the classic Grade III S. C. Gully (Ken Crocket).*

*The author on top of South Buttress, Stob Coire nan Lochan after soloing several routes in the same day (Ken Crocket).*

point, in February of that year I led SC Gully, cutting steps, in just under four hours. Two years later, front pointing with two axes, I made a roped ascent in one hour, admittedly in excellent conditions

Not that I personally went without the odd experiment. The second winter route I climbed (the first was a modest new route, 'disallowed' by the SMC!) was that of North-west Gully on Stob Coire nam Beith, in the freak icy winter of 1969. We climbed some steep pitches at the start, left of the normal, easy route. Near the top of the hard pitch on this I was so exhausted cutting steps that in desperation I front pointed the last section, using the axe and a peg hammer for balance. I vividly remember standing at the belay, pulling my fist open and watching it snapping shut with

cramp. My tiredness was probably responsible when, near the end of the route, the axe wobbled in my hand when cutting a step, and the pick hit me directly in the eye. A film of blood washed over the eye, my view of the world went rosy — and not so rosy — and I belayed to a spike of rock with the one good eye. Luckily it needed no treatment, and I was let off with a bloodshot eye for a week. In 1972, attempting Raven's Gully with Ian, and using his new, German ice hammer on the summer crux, I was almost over the chockstone and was in fact cutting the first hold in the snow above when the 'new technology' failed me. The slender pick of his hammer snapped and I was hurled backwards, undoing all the strenuous efforts of the last hour and a half. I somersaulted over the edge of the chockstone and swung to a halt opposite the belay, spitting mad.

## Failure

Two weeks after SC Gully I was back on Stob Coire nan Lochan with Colin, who was intent on climbing some horrific new line. We left Glasgow at 5.30 am on a beautifully clear and cold February morning, walking my new boots to the coire in 1 hour 20 minutes. This concern with the time taken to walk to crags had more than mere academic or egoistic interest; it was an indication of one's fitness, more important then than now, when front pointing the standard routes demands much less effort, stamina or time. The cliffs were as plastered in snow as I have ever seen them, a fairy-tale wall of castellated and brilliant white cliffs sparkling in the early morning sun. We were of course the first into the coire, its silent confines as yet unsullied by voices of the present. Voices of the past were in abundance; Raeburn and the Clarks on Central Buttress, Baird in SC Gully, Bell and Wedderburn, talented climbers all, their legacies before us.

The line which interested Colin has not yet been climbed, and details will therefore be suitably vague. Suffice it to say that I took one look at the narrow column of vertical ice oozing out of an overhang-topped chimney and shuddered. I belayed at its foot and watched him in action, paying out the ropes round my waist, no better system of belaying being available at that time. He had to cut steps in water ice, hanging on with one hand, spraying particles with every blow of the axe.

As his feet slowly climbed above my head I became aware that one of his crampons was detaching from his boot. Before this fault became a disaster, however, Colin saw the impossibility of his self-imposed crusade, and from about 20 ft up reversed back down, feet clicking into holds hard won from the ice. I shook my head when offered the lead, and we went elsewhere on the buttress and tried his second option of the day, a slightly less horrific line up a leaning wall coated with a sugary layer of snow.

I belayed to a deadman about 30 ft to the left, while Colin climbed on to a small ledge below the wall. At least I could see the possibility of this route, with ledges and grooves above, if only the initial steep wall could be breached. He placed a deadman runner in about 18 in of snow on the ledge, and stepped out right. A few moves up and he ran into terrible snow. A hold crumbled off the wall and he fell with it. I braced myself, aware of the terrible geometry of the ropes; a pull from the side on to a deadman was not praised in any textbook. The pull came and I was yanked off the stance, anxiously waiting for the outcome. To our amazement the deadman runner held as he flew through the air, landing in soft snow below the ledge.

We sorted ourselves out, exchanging worried queries regarding health, state of the belay and so on. To my amusement, once jangled nerves and tangled ropes were straight again, he set off back up the pitch. It was obviously going to be one of those determined efforts which so often singles out the good climber from the average climber. Today the conditions were against us though, and from near enough the same height he fell again, gear rattling through the air like a disastrous attempt at man-powered flight, to crash on the same landing spot. Again I was pulled off, and again the runner miraculously held, but we had reservations about a third attempt, a superstition with many graphic examples, and we called a halt. The irresistible had met the immovable.

The weather continued to be beautiful, if slightly mocking, and we salvaged the day with a burst of soloing. I, who had done no leading so far today, and as a consequence had less shattered nerves, soloed Pinnacle Buttress, Grade III. Colin accepted a rope for the crux bulge. Then we reversed the left fork of Forked Gully, soloed the right fork, descended

Broad Gully, and finally soloed Dorsal Arete, meeting on top for the third time a bemused climber intent on a more leisurely day. Excess adrenalin was finally flushed from our systems and we sat on top, satiated. We never did return to those lines, and they wait, ready for some young, strong pick-wielding ruffian who will no doubt wonder why they had never been climbed years ago...

## Success

The years had come and gone, and with them went step cutting and my innocence. Now front pointing ruled and the hills were over-run with a Gore-Texed babble; instant ice climbers with portable runners in each hand, praying mantis attacking the old routes with a new ferocity. Made old before our time we lurked in the quieter corners, avoiding the crowd, and so were small discoveries made.

In February 1976 I was climbing with Chris on Ben Nevis, drawn like a lodestone to its

**Far left** *Colin Stead attempts a new route on Stob Coire nan Lochan (although the exact location is secret!)* (Ken Crocket).

**Left and below** *Stuart Smith traversing out left on the exposed ledge of Harrison's Climb Direct, Ben Nevis* (Ken Crocket).

bewildering choice of climbs; never fully mastered as no great mountain can be. We had repeated some of the great classics and were now of the mind that hell is other people, so seeking a peaceful day we went under Carn Dearg Buttress to see what lay beyond. Colin and Dave lay beyond, standing at the foot of Waterfall Gully and looking slightly discomfited. Evening Wall, (which is what they were undoubtedly thinking of climbing that day) lay high above on the North Wall of Carn Dearg, its massive icefall prominent. (It was climbed at Grade V three years later.) I read the situation immediately and with Chris skipped past them to enter Castle Coire. We had no plans for the day. It was good enough to be somewhere different, somewhere unknown, and somewhere quiet on a mountain whose winters were no longer the playground of a privileged few.

Passing under the North Wall we came up to the foot of a steep, icy chimney. What it was we knew not, nor did we care. If looked fun and that was good enough, so we stopped and began the ritual process of gearing up. Done properly, slowly and in a familiar order, this routine hanging of harness and equipment can be made into a pre-climb meditation, a stilling of the mind, a preparation of the body. While we were thus engrossed my two old climbing partners appeared below, having decided not to attempt their line. There was obvious disbelief when we answered their query with the fact that we did not know the name of our intended climb, only that it looked interesting. I shrugged off their disbelief from my shoulders and turned to the chimney, wherein lay truth.

I had won the toss of the coin and the first pitch, up a steep and icy runnel forming a shallow chimney. It was not quite freezing here, though the ice was solid and clung to the picks with a reassuring familiarity. The first moves were the hardest, climbing absolutely vertical ice for several moves before it was possible to move into a slight lessening of the angle. A ledge system above and deep, soft snow allowed a belay to bring up Chris. The ledge led to a formidable-looking ice pitch in a corner of the wall, gained by an easy traverse over snow. I disallowed the easy traverse as a pitch, so that the ice pitch fell quite properly to Chris. Anyway I was content to share the load, and wanted to take photographs of the pitch, with its fantastic fringes of ice and

*Colin Stead on top of South Buttress, Stob Coire nan Lochan* (Ken Crocket).

downward-stabbing icicles. An aching distance above, on the huge wall of the buttress, enormous plates of ice threatened our vulnerable heads, bow waves on the flanks of the leviathan buttress. We tried not to think of their falling.

Chris had a relaxed attitude, doubtless nurtured during his previous experience of cave diving, a game which probably sorts out the men from the boys at a very early stage. His legs bridged up the vertical flutings of ice, the smaller icicles tinkling over the belay as he swept over them with his picks. It was now freezing, though whether this was due to a lowering of the general temperature or the miniscule increase in height was impossible to tell. At the top of the pitch Chris finished first on one knee, then both, and finally, to a barrage of amused ribbing from me, lying flat out on his stomach, feet projecting back out over the ice wall. When I came to follow, try as I did to avoid this inelegant manoeuvre, I was forced into exactly the same bizarre finish to the ice pitch, lying at full stretch in a

*The author on steep ice on Harrison's Climb Direct, Ben Nevis. In spite of new techniques, the rucksack is just as heavy and the ground just as hard* (Ken Crocket).

narrow, snow-filled gutter, picks flailing and failing. I laughed along with Chris as we looked up at the next section of the buttress.

We now found ourselves on top of what turned out to be Cousins' Buttress, a small, rounded buttress projecting out down and left of Raeburn's Buttress. The easy crest of the buttress led to the foot of a wall and the start of an exposed ledge which ran out to the left across the North Face. Above the ledge on the left stretched a barrier of steep ice, while on the right lay another buttress – Baird's Buttress, previously unclimbed in winter, as we later found. The honourable line lay up the left crest of Baird's Buttress, at the right end of the ice curtain, and I traversed out left in a truly Alpine situation; great walls above and below, no obvious way out, finally moving up and back right to belay below the rocky wall.

The nature of the climbing now changed, from the ice below to the rock and mixed ground above. It was turning out to be one of those great days which can rarely be planned in advance, when one is climbing well and the route is continually interesting and never too easy. Chris weaved a steep pitch up the unlikely looking buttress, finding a huge flake *en route* which almost promised a through route. I followed, impressed, to lead through on another mixed pitch to the gradually easing ground above. We had now climbed six pitches, of which only two had been done before; the ice pitch leading to the top of Cousins' Buttress, and the traverse pitch. We were happy, even enjoying the creeping muscle fatigue as we climbed the remainder of the buttress, taking an easy snow gully first recorded by Ian Clough to collapse on the summit of Carn Dearg. The Great Buttress was ours.

From the top of Carn Dearg the view to the south and west emphasized the superior height of Nevis. The February sun lay over Loch Lhinne, whose calm length lay glinting warmly below, with favourite hills holding the steel blue shadows of a winter unfinished. We reluctantly turned our backs to the sun and descended by the shadowy chasm of No 4 Gully, twisting down into the Coire of the Casket. In our hearts we too held a jewel or more, one of them just newly added. All of our February days had led to this February day, and we were content.

**Ken Crocket was born in Glasgow, where he now lives. After beginning with urban climbs, he progressed to local outcrops and then mountain crags. His first important ascents included Minus One Gully and Harrison's Direct on Ben Nevis, described above, and the Blackmount Wall routes on the Buachaille in Glencoe. He has written several books and is widely published in climbing journals. He likes to relax with yoga and music.**

# March: The Mad Month

## CAMERON McNEISH

I am not sure if I like ravens, I didn't like this one. He just sat there, like a vulture, watching and waiting. I was waiting too, and I was cold, very cold.

A thin rope snaked through my fingers, limply. It had been limp for over an hour and I longed to see it jerk into life. I prayed that I would open my eyes and see it slither through my Dachstein mitts as though it had come alive. I shouted again. No reply. Peter could be dead for all I knew.

My shout shifted the raven though. He shrugged his way into the air, grunting with indignation before settling on a ledge higher up the crag. I thought of throwing a stone at him, to try and clear him off, let him know I didn't like him. But I couldn't find a stone. Nothing but rocky slabs and ice. There was lots of ice, and that is what we had come for.

We had spotted it from the road, driving north to Glen Coe on a mad March morning of intense cold and black-iced roads. North of us great dark clouds brooded over the expanse of the Rannoch Moor and we knew it would be bad in Coire an Lochain and probably worse on the Buachaille. Then we saw the ice smear in Coire an Dothaidh. But it was comfortably warm in the car, with Christy Moore crooning huskily from the tape recorder, singing a song about Lisdoonvarna in County Clare, in the summer. It's a long, long way from Clare to here, or so the song goes.

You don't get 300 ft ice smears in County Clare, especially 300 ft ice smears that are only an hour's walk from the road, and with a good pub at hand for a couple of pints at the end of the day. It had looked like a promising idea. We couldn't resist it, until we got close to it and realized that it was very, very steep. Procrastination, as usual, won the day. We could warm up in a nice wee nearby gully, we thought. It looked easy enough, but Peter was stuck on the second pitch.

I had led the first pitch, a rope length of what turned out to be typical Cairngorm-style climbing; frozen turf with little snow to cheat with. It wasn't difficult climbing, but a build-up of snow would have helped. I found a belay below where the route disappeared from sight, over an arete, down an iced-up slab, and up a chimney to a large snow fan above. Peter climbed past me and led through, and that was the last I had seen of him.

'Is that Flasher you're on?' cried a voice from below. I got a bit of a fright because I was trying to outstare the raven at the time. You might get speaking ravens in County Clare but not in Coire an Dothaidh by Bridge of Orchy. A climber stood below me, staring upwards. 'Your mate looks as though he's stuck in a chimney.' Great, I thought, if Peter's stuck what chance have I got? He's as slim as a birch wand compared to me.

Now we had an audience of two and I definitely preferred the raven. At least he didn't give a running commentary. Peter, it seemed, had squeezed his svelte Welsh frame into the offending chimney, but could not raise his axes above his head because of lack of space. Neither could he step down back out of the chimney because his rucksack had caught on a runner.

The stranger seemed keen on conversation. 'It's only Grade II you know, but it might be a bit harder than that today because there's hardly any snow in it.'

Bugger off, I thought. It's annoying enough becoming stuck on what is supposed to be a 'wee warm up climb' without someone telling you it's only Grade II. The raven looked as though he was smirking.

The stranger moved off, having given all the advice he could, and as he vanished from sight a Welsh victory cry pierced the air, a cheer honed to perfection amongst the baritones of Cardiff Arms Park. The rope came alive.

Soon it was my turn to force cold stiffened limbs into action, to suffer that awful pain of blood returning to frozen fingers and knuckles as you batter then off hard ice at the ends of two ice axes. But at least I was moving. The front points of my crampons bit crisply into the thick water ice as I moved across the iced slab. Above me I could now see the narrow chimney where Peter had become stuck. Filled with snow it would have been a doddle, but today there was only the grim reality of grey granite, smeared here and there with delicate patches of water ice.

I didn't even try to squeeze. With the added confidence given by the top rope I climbed gingerly up the outside of the chimney, cramponed plastic boots poking and kicking at tiny rock holds. Peter smiled an embarrassed grin as I emerged on top of the chimney beside him, full of apologies for his delay. The rest of the route was dead easy but we had wasted a lot of time. March days are still treacherously short and by the time we had

---

*Climbing close to the rock so that we could find runners* (Cameron McNeish).

made our way to the base of the crags and had a bite of lunch it was half-past two and the sun was well down its mid-winter descent. The ice smear looked good though, and we thought we had time to have a good crack at it. 'We can always abseil off if we're beaten by the dark,' mumbled Peter.

His prophesy was spot on. We were barely half way up when the lights went out, or at least were dimmed enough to make us look at our watches. We had been thoroughly enjoying ourselves, concentrating hard on the iron hard ice. No simple kick here to gain a purchase from the crampon points, the ice was too hard for that. It was delicate climbing, holding on with three points of contact while a booted foot took careful aim. The axes barely went in more than half an inch, yet that was enough to allow progress. The route itself, first climbed by Ken Crocket who named it *Fahrenheit*, is a 200 ft ice smear which drops over a cliff or vegetated rock in a series of steep cascades. The smear can be taken directly, or by zigzagging from side to side, trying to find the points of least resistance. Since we only had two ice screws between us, we stayed close to the rock at the side of the smear where we could use rock runners for protection.

Peter led the first pitch, a steep ramp which led to the foot of the first technical pitch. As I belayed him I could see that the ice was very hard indeed. It took some time for him to hit a rhythm, and runners were hard to place on the broken and vegetated rock at the side of the route. But he managed to run out almost half a rope length before bringing me up. Using the nicks in the ice which he had made, I made quick progress and led through on to the first steep section, about 20 ft of 60° ice. Making sure I had our two ice screws I set off, trying to find axe placements high above my head. It was superb climbing and I was almost sorry when the angle eased off and I had to look for a belay. By the time I settled down and told Peter to climb when he was ready I realized that it was getting late and we would not finish the route in daylight.

We had a decision to make. Either continue on the route with the help of headtorches, or move off to the side and try and find a way down. I volunteered to look for a route down the less steep rock at the side of the route, and with Peter belaying set off, crampons sparking on the bare rock.

I soon realized that it would probably take us longer to try and find a way off the crag than it would to finish the route, so we compromised and decided to abseil off. A handy finger of rock gave a belay and we threaded the rope behind it and abseiled down, headtorches glaring and crampons knocking sparks off the rocks. It must have looked like a fireworks display from below.

Two rope lengths and we could scramble down to the snow fan where we had left our rucksacks. By this time it was pitch black, and the lights of the Bridge of Orchy Hotel away below us twinkled a welcome, giving us a longing to be somewhere warm and dry. It had been a full day and we were high with the sheer achievement of it. We hadn't done anything remarkable, but had enjoyed climbing within our limits in conditions which were varied and tested us in different ways. An hour later we were in the pub with a pint of beer in hand, laying plans to come back the next week and climb that big ice smear all the way. Boy, what we were going to do to it... But the next day it thawed and our ice route became a wee waterfall again. Such is the way of dreams and the reality of a Scottish March.

If Scottish conditions tend to be traditionally fickle for climbing snow and ice, it is often worse for skiers. I gave up the downhill Alpine variety as a serious proposition a number of years ago when the high octane promotion, the sheer volume of people and the notorious icy conditions of the Scottish ski piste made the cost of a ski lift pass appear unreasonable. So I took to Nordic skis, long thin steel-edged skis which, when the running surfaces are waxed correctly, can take you uphill as well as down, the ideal tools for exploring the Cairngorms and Monadhliath mountains close to where I lived for ten years in Speyside. Those years gave me a wonderful opportunity to enjoy these big hills, mostly in good weather, for being local you tend to pick and choose your days, often deciding on the spur of the moment to go out and make the most of it.

My first pangs of interest in cross-country skiing, borne of a desire to move more effectively through snow-covered country on hill walking trips and when walking in to far flung climbs, happily coincided with a revised interest worldwide in a cheaper, simpler form of skiing. In America, in particular, there was a growing anathema towards the growth of commercialism and the new flashy promotion of Alpine skiing, and disenchanted downhill skiers took to lightweight Nordic gear to slide off into the woods, the hills and the forests, far removed from the madding crowds of the pistes.

Inevitably the trend reached these shores, but it has been predominantly climbers and walkers who have taken up the challenge of Nordic ski touring, exploring the rolling terrain of some of our upland areas.

**Left** *Preparing to set off on a ski touring course in the Cairngorms* (Cameron McNeish).

**Far left** *Using Nordic skis it is possible to climb uphill as well as to slide downhill* (Cameron McNeish).

The ancient myth that you cannot turn on long, lightweight, Nordic skis has been well and truly exploded, and almost any day you can watch Nordic aficionados linking telemarks turn for turn with Apline skiers on the prepared pistes of Cairngorm and Glenshee. Indeed it is this age-old telemark turn, which was probably even used by Vikings, which has really revitalised Nordic skiing. The intricacies of the technique has been analysed and perfected by modern ski gurus and cross-country skiers are now tackling slopes which only a few years ago would have been avoided by everyone other than crack extreme Alpine skiers.

With Nordic and Alpine techniques and philosophy increasingly overlapping, the common ground shared by the two styles of skiing is becoming increasingly obvious. Tyro cross-country enthusiasts are using the uplift facilities of the Alpine ski resorts to practise their telemark techniques and downhill stalwarts are taking to the forests and hills on skinny skis when the pistes are out of condition. It is as it should be, two ski disciplines, making the best of each other's winter worlds.

Night-time skiing offers particularly memorable times, catching the full moon as it lights up the snow-covered fields and tracks making headtorches redundant. I have often stopped and watched the overhead drama of the northern lights, the aurora borealis, as it shone like a great floodlight across the northern skies. Other times we would stop and listen to the sounds of wildlife, often more noticeable during the dark nights of winter.

March is a good month to observe wildlife in the Highlands for the seasons are on the verge of change. Have you ever heard the bugling of wild whooper swans or the hag-like cackle of mallard through the stillness of a March night? It can sound eerie, especially when there is a blanket of snow on the ground to muffle the sounds so that it comes to you in an unfamiliar guise. With two friends, John and Taff, I went out one night and stood quietly by the shores of a still Loch Insh near to the village of Kincraig where I lived. The waters of the loch gently lapped against the snow-covered shore and the whooper sound was close. Because of the stillness the sound carried well, so the great swan could well have been in the nearby Insh Marshes which at that time were merely a flooded extension of the loch.

It was a great night to be out, the first wind-free night for long enough. Free of the scourge of gales, or lashing rain, or even driving snow, we had taken our cross-country skis and enjoyed a couple of hours kicking and gliding through the birch woods around the village. Although the sky was alive with stars there was no moon this night to light our way, so we made do with the harsh glare of headtorches, an eerie enough sensation in itself.

With only a pool of light immediately in front of us, we blundered on through the darkened woods, not entirely aware of when we were climbing uphill, or swooshing down long slopes until the backwards slipping of the skis, or the rush of air against our faces told us. One long and steep downhill was particularly exciting. One moment we were gliding along the flat, the next rushing downwards at speed. It was a fairly bumpy slope as slopes go and it was impossible to scan the slope ahead for difficulties as you would normally do in daylight. With the headtorches piercing the darkness only a few feet in front of us we had to try and judge the terrain through the soles of the skis, thinking through our feet if you like, hoping against hope that there was no great rock or tree stump lurking just below the snow surface. Strangely none of us thought of skiing it slowly and carefully, but we all came through unscathed. Taff managed to scuff a rock with the steel edges of his skis, a scuff which showered John and I in a flurry of sparks, like a steam locomotive crashing through the night.

Once again cross-country skis had showed me their worth during a spell when, despite a build up of snow on lower levels, gale force winds had kept the tops clear. But March is often a fickle month. She often comes in to

*Climbing on to Carn Ban Mor from Glen Feshie* (Cameron McNeish).

find the tops 'as bare as a bairnie's bum', but goes out leaving April to enter as a winter month rather than the harbinger of spring. What a country we live in. It drives you to the brink of despair time and time again and then surprises even the most pessimistic of us with a tapestry of glorious weather when we least expect it. It is days like that which make all the foul weather sufferable.

I recall one such day in the early morning, the sun just bursting over the long ridge of the Sgorans setting Glen Feshie alight, the overnight frost glowing orange, then pink as we drove up the long hilly road towards Achlean. Snow banked up on either side of road, glistened and sparkled as we passed. As we got out of the van the cold air nipped and hurried us into action, our breath hanging still in the air in front of our faces.

I had with me some members of a ski touring course which I had been instructing all week, and this was their last day. They had experienced the whole gamut of typical March weather in the previous four days of the course, from rain and slushy snow, to gale force winds and blizzards, and now it looked as though they could enjoy the best of it, sunshine and good snow. For the last four days they had been rehearsing for this day, their first real ski tour, not one that is going to push them to their limit, but a nice day of easy slopes, extensive views, good snow cover and maybe even a sun tan.

The Foxhunter's Path which runs up the broad flanks of Carn Ban Mor from Achlean to the Moine Mor, the Great Moss, was well and truly covered with fresh snow, and I broke the trail for the others to follow. It was hard work, but not as hard as it would have been walking. Footsteps would have been about knee deep, but the long skis spread the bodyweight evenly, and only sank in a few inches. It was tiring nevertheless, and hot work in the early morning sun. After half an hour we stopped

and started stripping off the layers, all those clothes that seemed so vital in the pre-dawn chill earlier. Twenty minutes later we stopped again, this time so that I could wax everyone's skis.

Modern Nordic skis come in two types, waxless, and waxable. Waxless skis have patterned indentations on the running surface of the ski sole, allowing the ski to grip the snow crystals as weight is put on the ski. This means that you can walk on your skis quite comfortably uphill. If you turn around and face downhill, the pattern of the indentations is such that resistance will be minimal, and the skis will slide down, hopefully taking you with them.

Waxable skis have a smooth running surface, and to create the necessary grip to climb uphill you have to rub a wax on to the ski sole. The advantage of waxing is that by using a wax which is co-ordinated to the temperature of the snow you can fine tune your skis to the prevailing conditions therefore achieving a better grip and glide. That is the rough theory anyway, but I suspect there is also a 'woodsy'

*Approaching the Great Moss with snow-covered hills in every direction* (Cameron McNeish).

**Above** *Sgurr Gaoith and the Great Moss, with ski tracks visible leaving the summit* (Cameron McNeish).

**Right** *Taking a break during a strenuous ski tour* (Cameron McNeish).

**Above right** *Telemark carves left on the smooth snow* (Cameron McNeish).

aesthetic appeal to waxing which many skiers find difficult to resist, a last defence, perhaps, against ever increasing automation and technology.

With our skis now gripping the snow surface satisfactorily, we made direct progress up the slope rather than tacking from side to side as we had being doing, which saves time as well as energy.

By this time the view was really opening up behind us, a splendid view down Speyside towards Laggan and beyond to where the great ramparts of Creag Meagaidh appeared shining white in the early sun. Beyond, just visible through a slight haze, the top spire of Ben Nevis rose above the neighbouring whaleback of the Aonachs.

These Glen Feshie hills are not by any means the most exciting in the Cairngorms, they are not the shapliest of hills and indeed they have been described by otherwise informed scribes as being uniformly dull. No towering spires here, no snow-plastered cliffs or castellated buttresses. But on a day like this they offer a subtle beauty.

Their curves accentuate the smoothness of the great snow fields, and their shadows cast a blue tint that seems to follow the lines of the furrowed gullies. Rounded and smooth there is a feeling of spaciousness, a bright glaring

world, harsh in its own way, and yet subtly gentle and welcoming. We soaked it in as though starved of such things, feeling the reflected sun burn our bare arms and faces. The sun tan of March comes quicker than the tan of June or July.

Climbing up towards Carn Ban Mor we dropped into a steady rhythm, the earlier chat now dried up, each lost in the effort of uphill plodding, knowing that soon we would be rewarded by downhill runs. The higher we climbed the more the smooth snow cover changed. Like frozen waves of the sea the great fields of *sastrugi* took our attention, marvelling at the beauty of it, and cursing the awkwardness of it. These waves are formed by the wind cutting grooves and patterns through the snow; terrible to ski on but incredibly beautiful, as though a storm lashed sea was suddenly put into deep freeze.

The Moine Mor, the Great Moss, was, as usual, breathtaking, a great panorama of glaring white topped by a wide blue sky. Ahead of us Braeriach raised its great head above its sculpted corries, and the great wedge of Sgurr Gaoith lifted itself into the sky from the plateau like a great slice of cake dripping with cream.

It is great to cruise effortlessly down the easy slopes from Carn Ban Mor, standing upright on the skis, no effort, no plodding, just free movement. Then gravity slowed us down as the downward slope merged into the uphill of Sgurr Gaoith, but the exhilaration of the downhill run stayed with us, encouraging, motivating, and we walked up Gaoith enjoying the Arctic splendour surrounding us.

The summit was fantastic. Perched on the very edge of the cliff the deep snow had covered the cairn and the cornice was huge. We took photographs of each other standing at the edge, standing on top of a white world with our ski tips sticking out over the void. Across Gleann Einich, Braeriach stood out boldly against a dark blue sky, each of its corries a gleaming snow bowl.

Another long run took us down the easy slope before climbing to the summit of Sgoran Dubh Mor. This was merely a peak bagging exercise for we had to return to the broad bealach for our route home, a broad ridge runs north westwards from the main Sgorans spine culminating in the top of Geal Charn. To reach it we had to negotiate a delightful slope. This slope always holds snow well into the season and always gives good sport. Today was no different. We really whooped it, linking tight telemarks in the fashion of slalom skiers, showing off to no-one and occasionally crashing without a care in the world. The snow was soft and deep enough to cushion the falls which was as well, for some of the falls were dramatic. Everyone was in high spirits, excited in the knowledge that it was all downhill to home. The hard work of the day was over, and unlike the hill walker who often suffers from plodding and knee-jarring descents, the ski tourer enjoys what is the highlight of the day.

We traversed the south flank of Geal Charn, just allowing the skis to run themselves, before dropping down to the natural funnel created by the time worn cradle of the Allt Ruadh, the Red Burn. Here was a natural ski run with a superb outflow, half a mile or so just allowing the skis to glide over snow-covered heather, not steep enough to require turns, or gentle enough to make you walk, just the right gradient to let the skis slide, enabling the skier to enjoy the surroundings completely at ease.

The sun was beginning to dip as we neared the ancient Caledonian Pines above Glen Feshie. The gnarled bark was reflecting the burnished red of the dying sun, and our faces were burning to match it. Time to take the skis

off and walk the remaining mile through the forest, stretching the legs and finding a few new bumps and bruises. Boy, we would be sore the next day!

But now and again, in this weird and wonderful and totally unreliable climate, there isn't enough snow for ski touring and spring has sprung early enough to strip the crags of snow and ice. I must admit to occasionally feeling relieved by an impatient spring. After long months of cold and the sterility of winter conditions it can be good to smell the earth again and to walk on grassy slopes. The first hill walks of spring can be refreshing, offering the freedom of unrestricted movement and the clarity of a new, vibrant season. I like to go somewhere new at the beginning of spring, and so I went to Glen Affric.

The constant drum roll that had filled my dreams all night long had ceased and I was being wakened by someone shouting. 'Look outside,' said the voice in my ear. 'It's as clear as a bell and the sky's blue.' My friend Hendy shook with excitement and a great grin was splitting his face. Realization dawned slowly. The rain had stopped and the wind was gone. In that semi-comatose state of half sleep I had spent half the night formulating plans for a low level wander in Glen Affric. But now the weather had changed and we were greeted by the sight of crystal clear sharpness and hills that etched their shape against a deep blue sky, dusted bright and fresh with new spring snow.

If anyone deserved a bonus we did. Just 24 hours earlier we had arrived in Gleann nam Fiadh, the Glen of the Deer, in a thick pea souper of a mist. The waters of Loch Beinn a 'Mheadhoin and Loch Affric had been as still as glass, grey and lifeless and reflecting all the dank depression of the morning. Although late March it was as mild and damp as August. Only the 'midgies' were lacking. We smelt wet, we felt wet, and the sound of a thousand cascades filled our ears. We found a dry island of turf and pitched the tent. It was only mid-morning.

After a brew and a change of socks we felt better. North of us, an ancient stalker's path wound its way up into a high corrie, from where it straddled a high bealach, the Bealach Toll Easa. On either side of this high pass were two Munros, Tom a 'Choinich and Toll Creagach, and Affric Tom n' Toll. As we waded up the track, which appeared more as a raging torrent, it was amusing to remember that this very path once connected two shooting lodges, Affric Lodge in the south, and Benula Lodge in the north. The latter is now submerged below the waters of Loch Mullardoch, the victim of hydroelectricity, although it would be easy to imagine that man had little to do with the flooding...

From the summit of the pass, a rough north-east bearing took us on and up a broad, featureless ridge. Toll Creagach seemed anxious to preserve any good features it may have for a better day, for it proved to be a dull plod to its triple cairned summit. Only a flock of some 50 or so snow buntings provided a distraction from the dripping grey shroud that enveloped us, and even the ptarmigan seemed loathe to shift themselves, still bright in their white winter coat, a useless camouflage against the unseasonal snowless terrain.

Tom a 'Choinich gave better sport; a steep scramble on a tight and narrow ridge. A beautifully engineered path of sorts avoided the greasy crags, and we enjoyed some interesting diversions trying to negotiate great snow fields, remnants of the last snow fall of some weeks before. From the bald pate summit of the hill, we took the south–east ridge of the hill as an alternative descent and thoroughly enjoyed the narrowness of it, skirting old and soggy cornices, peering into unknown depths where only the roar of waterfalls gave any indication of where the corrie floor was.

In the supercilious way that hill walkers have we told each other what grand fellows we were when we arrived back at the tent. How easy it would have been to miss out on the day. Instead we climbed two new Munros. Ahead of us lay a long night of drinking and gorging, chatting the evening away until a candle and a good book settled us for the night.

I have never known two days of such contrast. Instead of the dull sticky wetness of the previous day we had wakened to a crisp clear world. It was razor sharp, and the cold hurried us through the breakfast chores and into our gear. It was good to get moving, the colouring of red deer grasses emphasized by the brilliant snow dusting of the higher slopes and tops, a fresh breeze invigorating the spirit. Hendy, new to the winter hill game, was speechless with the wonder of it, showing his eagerness with a forced march along the floor of the glen.

Gleann nam Fiadh is a northerly offshoot of Glen Affric, and its river, the Abhainn Gleann nam Fiadh is Loch Beinn a 'Mheadhoin's major tributary. It is a tumultuous stream, made even more dramatic by the rain of the previous 24 hours. Great water slides scoured their way over the time-worn rocks, and a thousand cascades danced down the hillsides around us.

A great horseshoe of hills protect Gleann nam Fiadh, with two giants forming the head of the glen, Mam Sodhail, the Rounded Hill of the Barns at 3,862 ft and Carn Eige, the Cairn of the Notch, at 3,800 ft the highest point north of the Great Glen. Narrow exciting ridges form the connecting horseshoe, and our first task was to gain that ridge from the waterlogged glen.

An old stalker's patch carried us up in to Coire Mhic Fhearchair, and a stiff climb over rock terrain led us on to the ridge itself, on to the Garbh Bealach, the rough pass. Sadly our view to the north was spoiled by gathering clouds, a view that we had looked forward to with keen anticipation. The shores of Loch Mullardoch away below us had that artificial look of a pseudo reservoir, but even the dismal shoreline could not distract from the overriding impression that this was wild, wild country.

To the south the clouds were building up again too, dancing in and out and around the jumbled peaks, continuously flirting with the great ridges which seemed to radiate in every direction. The sun, however, was valiant, eager to show us the colours of this great tract of wildness. In the depths of the glens the slopes were rust red, swathed in great yellow tidelines which gave way to the white dusting of snow that had fallen overnight. Too cold to linger, we began to climb, the stalker's path reduced to anonymity below the fresh layers of powder.

Sron Garbh was the first top, and it gave some interesting axe work, its north–east ridge tight and steep, exciting in the swirling mists. At one point on the ridge our way was barred by a series of steep and jagged pinnacles, fine 'gendarmes' that tempted our scrambling instincts but sadly they were just too ice-bound for sport. Instead we negotiated a route through and around them, like Agag, treading delicately.

All too soon we were on Carn Eige, and we took shelter from the cold wind behind the wall that surrounds the triangulation pillar. Here we had a decision to make; whether we

should continue northwards to take in Beinn
Fhionnlaidh, or just carry on towards Mam
Sodhail. Fionnlaidh is one of these awkward
Munros that lie out on a limb. You either take
it in as an extra exertion on a natural round
like the Carn Eige/Mam Sodhail one, or else
you leave it for another day, another one
added to the list of 'odd' Munros that most
baggers finish up with. We left it. Even in
March the days are still comparatively short
and we still had a long way to go, back to the
tent and then the walk out to the public road
beyond Affric Lodge.

From Carn Eige the main road drops
south–west, the south across a high bealach to
reach the steep slopes of Mam Sodhail. This
summit was once an important survey station
in the primary triangulation of Scotland in the
1840s, and as a result boasts an astonishingly
large cairn. With the mist flirting around it, it
could well have been an ancient broch.

Three ridges emanate from Mam Sodhail,
and we followed the most northerly of them,
down over the Mullach Cadha Rainich towards
Sgurr na Lapaich, a delicately curving ridge
with steep flanks. We stopped for a while just
below the summit and watched great beams of
light pierce the clouds to spotlight great
chunks of hillside. It was almost like a stage
performance and we half expected to see some
rock group bounce on to the scene. It was
breathtaking, Scotland at her glorious best, and
we were sorry to leave. The day before we
had put up with poor conditions. Today we
had been rewarded for our patience. We
tramped down the glen in silence, collected
the tent, and went home, reaching the car as
darkness fell.

In the pale gloaming the ancient pines of
Affric stood like dark sentinels, the waters of
Loch Beinn a 'Mheadhoin were still and

*Ski touring in the Cairngorms above the Lairig Ghru*
(Cameron McNeish).

smooth, and flocks of chaffinches flickered
around us. It was tempting to stay, yet another
contrast to the conditions we had enjoyed
over the two days, the contrasts that make hill
bashing, whether on rock and ice, on ski or on
foot, such a glorious love affair.

**Cameron McNeish** is editor of *Climber Magazine* and lives in the small village of
Fintry in Stirlingshire, Scotland. He has written several books on outdoors
subjects and writes regularly for the Scottish press on outdoors affairs. He is also
a regular radio broadcaster and presents leisure programmes for BBC Radio
Scotland. He is an enthusiastic climber, hill walker and ski tourer and lists his
particular passions as winter climbing and 'long ski tours on good snow under a
blue sky'. Cameron is also a keen, but lousy, folk singer, and is a born again
Christian deeply involved in his local Christian Fellowship.

# April: A Yorkshireman Abroad

## DENNIS GRAY

Do you know the West Riding gritstone outcrops, Almscliff, Shipley Glen, Caley, Ilkley, Brimham and a host of others which serve the thriving climbing population of the Leeds/Bradford conurbation? Not as well known or lauded as their southern counterparts in the Peak District, they are, however, for sheer quality of climbing, centimetre by centimetre, metre for metre, the best climbing I have come across in 40 years of keen activity.

> 'Rock dark and look so heavily, your pebble pitted faces I know
> Lichen clings and greens merrily, rock for sun, the wind and snow'

Every year towards the end of March there is now in this modern era a frenetic spurt of activity on the ring of climbing walls that surround the area. At Leeds University, Guiseley, Rothwell and The Richard Dunn Centre in Bradford hosts of young people can be encountered, earnestly training, waiting, longing and hoping for April to arrive, with its light nights and the chance to be out in the open on mid week evenings once more. Almost like 'lifers' they have been encompassed in a cell, but sense that freedom can be theirs again once the spring is truly established. The spring was a long time in arriving in 1987 for the beginning of April heralded snow showers, high winds and heavy rain.

At Leeds University under the Henry Price building is a most unusual climbers' playground. Imagine a building set on stilts and these latter made of gritstone walls which are covered by the building itself, and which stop the rain from reaching the stone wall which is climbed. The wall is still set in the open air, but on the stones used by climbers faces almost east, and is therefore protected from the prevailing westerly winds which come sweeping across the Woodhouse Moor. Occasionally if the wind is in the east it can be too cold to climb there in the mid-winter but

*Ilkley Quarry, West Yorkshire, is a place full of happy memories* (Dennis Gray).

*The wall at Henry Price Building, Leeds University* (Dennis Gray).

in early April it is always possible. It is the best finger and forearm training I know of and the four walls, which are actually the retaining walls of the old Woodhouse Cemetery, give a possible continuous climbing of over 120 metres. Each of the four walls has a different degree of difficulty, and they are separated by a doorway which can also be traversed. The easiest wall, the number two, is continuous 4C, number one is 5A/B, number three is 5C and the fourth wall is 6A. That is working from left to right. If you are strong you can climb the whole of the second wall using only smears for your feet, but that requires some local knowledge as well as strength and good footwork.

The whole is set in a graveyard and is lit up at night-time so that even at midnight one can still see sufficiently to do some climbing. It is eerie to be there alone in early April at 9 o'clock at night in the dark, especially as the graveyard is a favourite spot with local drunks who like to sit supping behind the grave stones. On occasion after imbibing more than usual they have been known to emit screams or high-pitched cackles, usually as one is

reaching for a small side hold with a single foot on a small edge. Such a scream piercing an ill-lit night can cause even the strongest to waver! (I had better explain that Henry Price is a hall of residence hence the night lights, which are not to keep the ghosts and drunks at bay.)

In those first days of April 1987 with its ghastly weather, the British Mountaineering Council, for whom I work, was acting as the host to the UIAA Technical Commission meetings at Leeds University for almost a whole week, so I was able to spend time training on The Henry Price in between these gatherings and the associated social events.

On the first Monday in April I had to be in Paris for a meeting at the French Sports Ministry. This provided the excuse to load my car with two members of the Leeds University Mountaineering Club, Matt and Joe, and head for a weekend's bouldering at Fontainbleau, that superb sandstone area approximately 30 miles south of Paris. Matt is a medical student, large and very amiable whilst Joe is reading philosophy, a mature student from Liverpool but born in Italy and built like the proverbial brick barn so we were an unusual mix. It was a harrowing drive on the Friday night, with pouring rain and a near crash in the fog due to a broken windscreen wiper in which I almost collided with one of those trailer-truck juggernauts which seem to fill the road on the south side of Paris. This made sure my passengers kept talking and did not fall asleep on me. Arriving at the camp site near to Cuvier, one of the best climbing areas situated just off the N7, we had the tent up and were into our sleeping bags before you could say 'Voulez-vous se coucher avec moi?'!

Fontainebleau is, apart from West Yorkshire, the best bouldering I know. A former Royal Hunting forest covering hundreds of square kilometres it is at its most beautiful in the spring and autumn, and over the years I have been there many times with assorted companions. It is a complicated area geographically and finding the different climbing sites can be very difficult. First time visitors are recommended to purchase a guidebook. Despite many visits I still get lost in the forest, especially if visiting one of the more remote outcrops of which there are over 30.

If there for any length of time you must visit the village of Barbizon for it has a place unique in the history of art, and still has some of the finest galleries to be found outside the major conurbations. (Less high-minded climbers might like to visit the bars and 'caves' in Fontainebleau town itself where it is possible to purchase in the latter wine at prices which seem ridiculously cheap.) The chateau at Fontainebleau is one of the most famous in France and is a national monument.

On our visit in April 1987 the weather was not its usual French self and we woke on the Saturday morning to heavy rain pattering down on the tent. My companions were heading south on the Monday to Buoux and Verdon, and I teased them that there would be snow in those regions at this time of year. Joe had spent a whole week bouldering at Fontainebleau the previous year, quite a feat in itself and a tribute to the stamina and hardness of the skin on his fingers. The rock there is hard sandstone not unlike gritstone, with intrusions of small volcanic flakes, the 'grattons'. Over the years a school of climbing based on these outcrops has evolved, and many of its pioneers such as Pierre Allain, Jaques de Lepiney, Robert Paragot and moderns like Jacky Godoffe are amongst the great names of French

mountaineering. You must be prepared for 'Bleau and you need a piece of carpet to take off from to keep the sand off your rock boot soles, a rag to keep your feet clean, colophon (resin) in a poff bag, besides shorts and sticky boots. The original rock boot, the PA, was invented by Allain for Fontainebleau, became the EB and led on to all the modern boots which we have today. It is a sobering thought to realize that these were developed in 1946, the year before I began to climb! It is possible to wander in the woods all day and barely meet a soul, whilst during weekends at the popular climbing outcrops like Dame Jehanne it can be like being on a crowded beach with so many people about.

A late start took us down in to one of Joe's favourite bars in the town, which turned out to be vastly overpriced. But as Joe informed us, this was no outing for tight fisted Yorkshiremen, but more an investment for our future for here to be found in abundance in the evenings were the best looking girls this side of Paris!

Miracle of miracles! Alors, le soleil! We had not seen anything like it for six months and the steam began to rise from the pavements outside the bar. Time to go back to the camp site for Joe to cook us one of his Momma's specials, Spaghetti tutti frutti. By early evening it was dry enough to climb and we chose to go to the area of the Gorges d'Apremont. I had never been there before and this was Matt's first visit to 'Bleau, but Joe had everything under control and seemed to know every worthwhile move and every problem. I was definitely the twerp of our side for a week earlier I had fallen off the top of the Leeds University Wall and hurt my left kneecap so badly I dare not try anything I might have to jump down off. This was a definite disadvantage at 'Bleau where you often have to take great leaps off the boulders before you find the correct hold sequence before climbing. The circuits are graded in different colours according to difficulty; orange, green, blue, red, white, black, some of which are very famous such as the blue circuit at Malesherbes, the red circuit at Roche Sabots and Trois Pignons, the white circuit at L'Elephant and the black at Cuvier. These are in ascending order of difficulty and to climb the white or black problems you have to be very fit and technically brilliant. Needless to say my companions were intent on the white or black problems! I wandered off on my own and enjoyed climbing some blue and occasional red routes. I did manage one single white at Apremont but was petrified in case I had to leap off from the top. Most of the landings at 'Bleau are good and some of the outcrops such as L'Elephant or Trois Pignons are set in sandy deserts and you would be very unlucky to hurt yourself at such sites, but at the Gorges the landings are tricky and I kept a low profile.

That night we tucked into our sleeping bags on as fair an evening as one could wish for in April. Cold, very cold, but a sky to savour with every star twinkling and winking at us promising a great day for the morrow. We would then go to Cuvier perhaps the most famous of all the outcrops, nearest to our camp site and the road, and well-known to Joe and myself. There are to be found the most classic problems at 'Bleau and some of the hardest and most famous in France, La Joker, L'Abbatoir, Le Carnage, La Marie Rose, Big Boss. Once again we awoke to rain drumming on the fly sheet of the tent. This was just too much and we felt hard done to, despite the steady stream of earthy jokes emanating from Joe who was by now getting wet as the wind was blowing the rain into his side of the tent. Mercifully it began to clear up and within minutes a hot sun had us out of the tent for a lesson from Matt in juggling! Despite having to travel light for his long hitch south, with no food, no stove and no cooking pans or tent etc he had brought his jugglers clubs! There is dedication for you, and the French climbers on the camp site were impressed as he threw them between his legs, around his body, up into the air, catching them in unison.

Soon we were down at Cuvier and we climbed until late that evening. Hot sunshine, shorts and T shirts, classical 'Bleau conditions. There were dozens of climbers there and if you want to see bouldering action go to Cuvier on a Sunday for the 'Bleaussards who do go there are the best around and they have most of the boulder problems down to a fine art. One suspects they could climb them blindfold, and certainly some of them are reminiscent of concert pianists playing their favourite passages from memory. Five or six hours climbing at Cuvier is enough to take the skin off anyone's fingers. The 'super grattons' are like razors and by the late Sunday evening we had exhausted our desire to climb. Bidding goodbye to my companions the next day I attended at the

Ministre de Sport et Jeunesse in Paris then drove home, after an eventful weekend.

Work then intervened for a few days but the following Sunday was the first good day of Spring. I travelled out from Leeds about 12 miles to Shipley Glen, a gritstone outcrop near to the town which had rightly become immensely popular since the publication of the Yorkshire Gritstone Guidebook in 1982 which included for the first time a full guide to the crag by Mike Hammill. Like many other West Yorkshire climbing grounds Shipley Glen was a close guarded secret for generations. I first climbed there in 1952 with my mentor Arthur Dolphin and have been a regular visitor ever since. It is quite simply a brilliant place to visit and to climb solo and there are now 120 routes of between 15 and 30 feet in height. A young friend of mine actually climbed all of them in one day, all the more remarkable

**Left** *Apremont Gorges, Fontainbleau* (Dennis Gray).

because at that time he was only sixteen! The standards at The Glen tend to be high, but the problems are beautiful. The crag faces almost South, is sheltered from the wind and it is a must as soon as the weather improves, and the mere mention of some of the climbs — Scoop Arete, Manson's Must, Austin's Hangover, Piton Rib (which I made the first ascent of in 1952 and called Kia Ora, but which Ian Clough subsequently pegged!)—makes the fingers itch to get out onto the grit again. Easter was now fast approaching and after the usual round of meetings, telephones, letters and problems at the Council I escaped for a few days with my two sons, Stephen and Robin, and a young friend, Bjorn, to North Wales.

There is something divine about youth, and when you are middle-aged and beyond to be in the company of juvenile climbers is to relive days that you have forgotten. It helps one to remember how you felt about going away at Easter and packing your rucksack, the first real holiday of the year. Young climbers nowadays have more free time, more equipment and more money than we ever did, but they are still the same; the eager excitement as we were driving down to Snowdonia, the keenness to get out onto the rock faces, the laughter and banter as we put up the tent, and the disappointment at finding the rock face wet on our arrival at the foot of the climbs were all familiar.

Because it had been wet for days before our arrival, we had decided to travel down to Tremadog, hoping that the hot sun which now pertained would dry out the crags there quickly because of their aspect. But weeks of wet weather had meant that it would take longer than a few hours to achieve this task, and as I led my youngest son Robin, 14 years old, up Y Broga on Craig Bwlch Y Moch I slipped around on the greased rock as I climbed up the first crack. Bjorn and Stephen were climbing Gurr-Eagle; no easy task as the ramp was wet, and as I looked down on Bjorn from above him on the stance of the second pitch of Y Broga I could see he was not too happy struggling with the conditions. Somehow he coped and reached the top with the support of a few encouraging instructions. Stephen, however, had not climbed for six months and managed to fall off the crux seconding and was lowered spiralling through space unceremoniously to the ground. This was not surprising really, for he had not touched rock all winter, having spent his time rehearsing or playing Shostakovitch's 9th, Berlioz's Symphony Fantastique or gigging with friends from his music school in their rock band at such high-faluting venues as Wigan Tech! It took the boys ages to sort themselves out and it was dark before they managed to retrieve all the equipment and the pair of them had returned to the camp site. When you are seventeen such adventures are the spice of life.

Tremadog is a surprising place and when I first visited it in 1956 I would never have imagined it would have become popular. Climbing with a school friend, Brian Evans, we had spent all day on Olympic Slab and Belshazzar and we lost so much blood fighting through the brambles that we called the place Dracula's Cliff. There were no paths and no detailed guide book, and finding the few climbs that had been pioneered was a major feat in itself. Our ascent of Belshazzar must have been an early one, and I remember whilst leading, pulling over the overhang on the first pitch hanging on by a slender tree route. At Easter 1987 I looked for this but now all that remains is a clean sweep of rock. This is the story of the whole Tremadog escarpment which is in all truth four separate cliffs spread out over several miles. Craig Bwlch y Moch is owned by the BMC whilst Craig Pant Ifan is held by the Nature Conservancy Council on a lease. Both of these two crags are SSI's, but the rare plants are to be found in areas of the cliffs unused by climbers, and many years of experience have shown that nature protection and cragging can co-exist without detriment to either. The rock is beautiful dolerite (rather like gabbro) and despite being close to the road and almost having an urbanized feeling

whilst climbing there, the quality of the climbing is outstanding. Most climbs are in the 200 ft height category and there are routes of every grade of difficulty.

Good Friday was a superb, hot and sunny day and we believed that we were set for a beautiful Easter. So did dozens of other climbers who were also on the rock faces and queuing to climb became the order of the day. This is a modern phenomenon which would have been unthinkable in, say, 1956. It is also, I believe, potentially dangerous and I do know of a couple of incidents where climbers waiting to climb have been hit ether by falling rocks dislodged from those above them and or in one case by a falling climber. In one tragic case in Derbyshire a young climber was killed in such circumstances. The only answer seems to be to go somewhere unpopular at holiday times, and two days later I was to find the outcrops at home in West Yorkshire were deserted!

It is both enjoyable and immensely satisfying to climb with your own children, but it can

*Superb sandstone at Cuvier, Fontainbleau* (Dennis Gray).

also be extremely worrying if you see them having difficulties whilst leading on climbs not too well protected. It is therefore not easy to relax with them on difficult climbs. I opted to climb mostly with Robin and led him up Creagh Dhu Wall, Valeries Rib and some other easy routes. I also climbed Scratch Arete, Grim Wall Direct and Itch with Bjorn, on which he was feeling his way, having climbed very few routes in North Wales. Stephen and he did climb several respectable routes, including Pincushion, but the weather rapidly deteriorated on us. Even a visit to Jim Perrin who had recently moved back into the area for an exile's return to his beloved North Wales, failed to keep the rain and storms at bay. By Sunday evening it was like the days of old when we used to camp as young boys in the Llanberis Pass and when I was Joe Brown's gentleman's gentleman. My task used to be to hold on to the tent poles all night, but that was before the modern lightweight tents with their sewn in ground sheets.

We were soon getting wet, so we decided to vote on what to do. Democracy is a fine thing! Three of us voted to pack up and retreat to West Yorkshire where the sun always shines, whilst Robin with the enthusiasm of extreme youth kept insisting it would soon clear up! We packed up and drove through the night back to the land of the giants and it rained every inch of the way — which was dammed unfortunate as I still had not managed to find time to have my windscreen wipers mended! My eyes are still aching from peering through the windscreen into the rain and murk. It was with true relief I reached my house back in Leeds.

By lunch-time the next day it had stopped raining but was very cold. The weathermen said it was the coldest Easter Monday for years, but it was just right for a visit to Caley. If you have never been to Caley Crags 8 miles from Leeds on Otley Chevin (there are three outcrops in all there and a quarry) do not delay, go there today. There are climbs such as Noonday Ridge, Lad's Corner, and Vampire's Ledge which would be classics anywhere, and

_Froggatt's Edge is one of many places in Derbyshire where people flock to perfect their techniques_ (John Woodhouse).

there are also the 'big' modern hard routes such as The Great Flake and Adrenalin Rush. But it is for the boulders that you should go. They are exquisite and along with Almscliff give the finest problems I have ever come across. For some reason bouldering does not fit into any prerequisite weather syndrome, except that it does not require it to be too hot. It is best at about 6 to 10° once you are warmed up thoroughly, and at places such as Caley cool windy days after wet spells give superb friction. We climbed until our fingers were sore and always it is a delight to take someone there who has never been before and show him as we did with Bjorn, the intricate problems that abound all over Otley's Chevin. Many of the boulders are high enough to hurt yourself if you fall off, but never once did our young apprentice falter, so we rounded the evening off with a hot curry and a large bottle of wine at my home in the Leeds 6 climbers' ghetto.

The next day was spent at Ilkley. My two sons had to return to their studies but Bjorn and I had a simply superb day as the weather steadily improved. We never once used a rope and many of the routes at the outcrop we soloed. Some say Ilkley Quarry is an 'old boot of a place' but it is for me a spiritual home. I started climbing there when I was a very small boy and to go there and feel the wind on my face as I walk into that place is to recall so many memories and so many friends, now unfortunately no longer with us. Such as Authur Dolphin, Eric Metcalfe, Ian Clough, so many days of magic and friendship, and it will always remain for me a special place. To climb well there you need strong fingers and despite its run–down appearance there are some fantastic climbs. Botterill's Crack is still a test piece (yes! this is by the one and only Fred who was of course a Leeds Lad), so is Dolphin's Highfield Corner, Austin's High Street, Livesey's Wellington Crack and Fawcett's Milky Way. To climb at Ilkely is to be in touch with British outcrop climbing as it has developed over almost a hundred years. Still new routes are appearing and John Dunne's impressive Snap Decision to the right of Wellington Crack is a recent addition which brings the story right up to date. We climbed in the Quarry and on the rocks outside the Cow and Calf then Olicana Buttress. We climbed until we could stand it no more. I have often read about climbers who have kept

*Stephen Gray on Adrenalin Rush, Caley Crags, West Yorkshire* (Dennis Gray).

climbing with their fingers bleeding but never before have I witnessed this and Bjorn climbed with blood streaming from his digits. It was time to go home and back to work for a rest!

The weather was now superb with the hottest April days for 20 years. But work had to come first so in my frustration I went out one evening before a late night meeting for a run. My kneecap had still not recovered from the fall I had taken the previous month and as I hobbled round the streets of Manchester in a heat wave I could feel the stares of sympathy, especially when one lady actually overtook me at a brisk walking pace. It transpired she was hurrying to catch a bus!

The last weekend in April was the BMC AGM and dinner in Keswick. I took my two boys

with me and my daughter Helen. Unlike the boys she has never really taken to climbing and although now almost 12 she is still tiny. It is very difficult to climb when the holds are so far apart! On the Saturday the four of us took ourselves off down Borrowdale to Shepherd's Crag. Like Tremadog in Wales if anyone had told me on my first visit there in 1952 that it would become one of the most popular cliffs In Britain I would not have believed them. We had low opinions in those days of roadside crags for we did not believe the quality of the climbing compared with the magnificent cliffs of Scafell or Snowdon. However, to be fair Shepherd's was never as vegetated as Tremadog and I can recall how much I enjoyed climbing routes like Eve and Ardus the first time I ever ascended them. My two sons climbed together whilst I led my daughter up Brown Slabs and then Donkeys Ears. We could not get rock boots small enough for her so she had to climb in her gym pumps and how that brought back memories! I soloed Fishers Folly and another route at the side of Kransic Crack, then my son Stephen led me up Eve. I thought of my friend Bill Peascod as I followed that

**Left** *Climbing at Ilkley* (Dennis Gray).

**Below** *Cow and Calf Rocks, Ilkley* (Dennis Gray).

route. He had made the first ascent almost 40 years earlier and what a great pal he had been. We had first met on Castle Rock in 1952 when I had been with Arthur Dolphin. He had been a Vice President of the BMC up until just before his death on Cloggy in 1985. We raced back to Keswick where I was just in time for the BMC AGM, held in the late afternoon.

The Council has been my life for the last 15 years and I do feel that I have been extremely lucky to be involved in working for something more than a sport which is a way of life that means so much to me. The AGM was followed by the dinner and it was marvellous to see so many faces there, young and old, a cross section of British climbing. In the bar was Doug Scott and it only seems a few years ago that he made some of his first climbs with me when a schoolboy in Nottingham. I recall epics in the winter on Craig yr Wysfa, Moss Ghyll on Scafell and on Cloggy. But that is another story. The carousing finished in the early hours of the morning, and our climbing next day despite the superb weather was very low key. We opted for the Bowderstone Area and after parking the car walked past the quarry (now blown-up) where Ken Russell shot his famous Mahler dream sequence and along the path to the Bowderstone. Through lush vegetation, rhododendron, azeleas, and bracken. We bouldered on the stone then moved off and Stephen took Helen up Woden's Face whilst I soloed that and two other routes on the buttress. We then walked down to the river Derwent. Everywhere looked at its best; with a cloudless sky, the bird song, insects, yes April had at last brought a true spring and life back to this, the most beautiful of Lakeland valleys.

We were brought back to earth as we hit the traffic jams travelling home, first down the M6 to Manchester to drop Stephen at his school. Then across the Pennines back to Yorkshire. I have been accused of being a professional Yorkshireman but do not care! For on the last evening of the month, after work and driving home the 40 miles from Manchester I travelled out to Caley Crags to the Sugerloaf area. Arriving about 8 o'clock it was obvious that something was in the air. The hot weather could not last much longer so I resolved to make the most of it. With a friend Stephen (not my son), the Secretary of the Leeds University Club, I stayed out climbing until dark. As the sun went down it was magnificent. Rays of

light splayed out over Wharfedale, the home of my father's forebears, for he was born and bred down the road in Otley just ten miles from Leeds. How I love these rocks and this area. I have lived in India, in Kenya, in Scotland, the Lake District and on the edge of the Peak, but my heart is there. To be at Caley Crags on Otley's Chevin on a fine April evening, either in company of a gregarious bunch of climbing friends or wandering alone around the boulder fields is for me a joy that never fails to satisfy. At other times of the year it can be equally joyful but the fact that April is the start of a new climbing season with those long light nights to look forward to makes it the most special month of the year for me and each year it marks a new beginning, with old and new friends.

The winters in the north of England are in the main cheerless months, and anyone who has worked outside either instructing mountaineering, working on the land or merely travelling around the country will know how keenly those who have such tasks to perform do look forward to the spring. After 40 years of climbing, my days of sitting on wet ledges and climbing cracks with water pouring over me are not so frequent as they once were; in fact in all truth I try to avoid

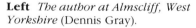

**Left** *The author at Almscliff, West Yorkshire* (Dennis Gray).

such conditions. Thus each winter I look forward with keen anticipation to April, for it is possible to make a fresh start, to begin again and who knows I may yet one day at such a beginning go out to Caley, to Almscliff or to Ilkley and all those problems I have never been able to climb, I will cream them all! Yes, April is a month when even the impossible dreams do sometimes come true.

A few days later I was out at Almscliff and the impossible was happening 40 years after starting to climb. I was ascending problems as hard as I had ever done and one I had never been able to climb before. Just before packing in for the evening I was powering up a difficult little route when my hands slipped from off a pinch and ...

> Falling
> Texture of the wind crashing
> Into a million facets of
> me;
> Am I making the wind?
> Or was it always there
> Can I catch it?
> Get ahead of it into the stillness?

I hit the ground with a gasp as a rock sank into my spine. No serious damage, but two baths a day and a lot of pain were to be May's story whilst April had been one of joy.

---

Dennis Gray was born in Leeds in 1935. He began climbing in his native West Yorkshire in 1947, and since then has been a member of four expeditions to the Himalayas and one to the Andes, as well as climbing in many other parts of the world. He is a former president of the Karabiner, Rock and Ice and Leeds University climbing clubs, General Secretary of the British Mountaineering Council and a member of the Alpine Club. He is also a voluntary student counsellor in Leeds. He plays the tenor banjo badly, sings even more poorly and is a slow runner, failed poet, wit and raconteur, and drinker of Tetley's bitter.

# May: The Rites of Spring

## BILL O'CONNOR

Spring, when a young mountaineer's fancy turns to ... Nepal!

April and May are a good time to be in Nepal. For me the long winter months and hard driving in search of snow and ice take their toll and the masochistic me gives way to a softer self and a longing for a bit of tropical warmth.

When you step off the plane in Kathmandu, usually overladen; in an attempt to get through all your extra gear as hand luggage, the subtropical sun invades you making completely redundant that extra sweater and duvet jacket. All of those heading for high places seem to be dressed in similar fashion; 20 kilo is obviously not enough for the international jet-trekker! By the time you have identified your luggage and sweltered through customs, the phrenetic hubbub of the taxi rank and dubious safety of the dilapidated vehicle are a welcome haven.

*The ice fall and headwall leading to the col on the south-west ridge* (Bill O'Connor).

**Above** *Dawn on the peaks of the Nepal Himalayas, seen from the rim of the Kathmandu Valley near Nargakot* (Bill O'Connor).

**Left** *Taweche and Cholatse emerge from morning cloud above Pheriche* (Bill O'Connor).

That first day in Kathmandu is always a little heady. Spaced-out on jet-lag and airline fast food the mystical atmosphere of this wondrous capital acts like a narcotic for some as they wander along crowded alleys amongst hectic street life, entwined with the deities of Hindu, Buddist and animistic faiths. Things that seem magical to the westerner mingle with the mundane in Kathmandu.

What Kipling said of it holds true:

> Still the world is wondrous large
> Seven seas from marge to marge –
> And it holds a vast of various kinds of
>     man,
> And the wildest dreams of Kew are
>     the facts of Kathmandu
> And the crimes of Clapham
>     chaste at Martaban.

The spring months of April and May in Nepal have always been good to me. I had been in Nepal for the autumn. After more than two months of trekking and climbing in the Jugal and Langtang Himals, following routes pioneered by Tilman, even Casius would have looked rotund by comparison. I was on my way to Kala Patar to have a look at a possible route on Pumori when I met up with members of the American Medical Research Expedition that had just climbed Everest. Amongst them was Jeff Lowe with whom I had climbed in Colorado. As we chatted in a T-House near Pheriche, Peter Hackett who had solo summited from the South Col, spoke of his spring plan to return to the Khumba to attempt a 'first ascent' of Cholatse, the last major unclimbed peak in the Everest region.

The first time I saw Cholatse, several years before, my dreams were captured by it. Viewed from the main Everest valley or from the valley of the Ngozumpa Glacier near Gokyo it is a superb fang of rock and ice. At this time I had assumed that it had been climbed, it was such an obvious prize. My first researches also led nowhere since the peak on the Swiss Scneider maps is called Jobo Lhapsan, a name that not even the Sherpas know it by!

Despite his emaciated condition and a couple of broken ribs sustained in a fall from the Hillary Step, Peter enthused about this, the 'last virgin in the Khumbu', explaining how it was to be an all-American expedition. Disappointed at this news and envious of their chance, I

*Roskelley and Ang Nima take a look at the as yet unclimbed Cholatse* (Bill O'Connor).

wished them well. At the time I did not realize how much the mountain had come to mean to me and how I did not want them to succeed on the climb, hoping instead that I could get permission for an attempt.

Two months later I was in California when I met Peter Hackett again at the house of a mutual friend. Cholatse raised its beautiful head and Peter asked whether I still fancied having a go at it. It seemed as luck would have it that Jeff Lowe was unable to get away because of work commitments and that nationalism gave way to friendship, and the American Cholatse Expedition was about to become an Anglo-American one.

With less than eight weeks to go Peter said

he would be in touch, in typical laid-back west coast style. Five nail–biting weeks later a letter arrived saying to meet in Kathmandu! It is strange to reflect how one person's 'laid-backness' can lead to panic and uptightness in others!

To date, however, the expedition was fulfilling Tilman's dictum of 'on the back of an envelope' since that was about all the information I had regarding the who, what, when or where of it. In the end we met up at the house of Al Read in Kathmandu. The room was full of bronzed faces, some recognizable and the heady, exotic smells of Nepal mostly unrecognizable. Pale from jet travel and the English winter I went through the ritual of even more laid-back introductions. Peter and Al I knew. The others I also knew but only by reputation: Galen Rowell whose books and photographs give superb insights into American climbing both at home and abroad. His was a short muscular frame topped by a mass of black hair. With very short legs and abnormally long arms he looked like a sophisticated neanderthal. Galen it seemed was just off to lead a group of 'mail-order' mountain photographers around the Sherpa villages, thus paying for his trip and hopefully getting him fit into the bargain. From a shady alcove a huge hand at the end of a powerful arm emerged and engulfed my own limp offering. Lantern jawed and every inch – or should it be foot – of him a Californian rock jock. The arm belonged to a body that should have belonged to muscle beach, but in fact belonged to Vernon Clevinger who would have been at home equally on the beach or on a mountain. The 'hulk' as he later became known was our secret weapon; if we couldn't climb it, he could pull it down! From the brightest corner of the room shone the mischievous self-assured smile of one of the world's leading Himalayan mountaineers; John Roskelley. With a reputation for hard climbing and an awkward personality; happy to speak his mind, John has a bit of a red-neck image, fostered through his love of hunting, a belief in the right of every American to own a gun and his habit of chewing tobacco! However, he remains the author of many fine climbs with ascents of K2, Makalu, Trango Tower (the real one) and the audacious Uhli Biaho to his credit. With credentials like that it really came as no surprise to find that his mother was a GI bride from Yorkshire. Thus he was duly co-opted into the Anglo camp; that is we shared a tent!

Peter, an emergency doctor, had things organized having spent much of the last eight years running the Himalayan Rescue Association hospital in Pheriche and becoming an authority on high altitude medicine, a fairly rarefied occupation! The food loads were already being portered into the Everest region, whilst we were to fly to Lukla in a couple of days' time where the aim was to wander for a week or so up the Dudh Khosi Valley, meet with old friends amongst the Sherpas and enjoy their inevitable hospitality of chang and rakshi, and so eventually end up at the foot of the mountain.

The expedition was to be a low key affair in every way. No last great problem hype, just a small group of committed climbers enjoying a climbing holiday.

The week wandering in the Khumbu was a lot of fun, although I am not sure how much it contributed to our acclimatization. We wandered to Thyangboche for the Rimpoches blessing, and a lot more chang. At a small T-House run by the wife of IlaTaschi, a respected Sherpa, Sardar, an older Sherpa, related a story about Sagamartha or Mt Everest, the Mother Goddess of the Earth, about how the mountain had five sacred daughters that included Cholatse and of our good fortune and karma that we should be going to climb her. It seemed that the vibes were good. Only the weather needed to improve. It is quite normal in late April and May for the weather to be hot, especially at lower altitudes. Higher up, the morning sky tends to be clear but hazy, without the sharp clarity of the post-monsoon period. By mid-morning big cumulus had filled the sky and the high peaks were only glimpsed through the clouds. Whilst we were wandering through 'sherpa-land', light snowfall sometimes dusted the higher yak pastures and whitened the normally black rock buttresses.

By mid April four of us with our Sherpa Sardar, Ang Nima and cook Pemba set up Base-Camp in a Yak pasture at 15,500 ft below the west face of Cholatse. Along with three dome tents, the spoils of the Everest expedition, we also had a huge blue mess-tent as a general store and meeting and eating place. At this time Galen was still wandering the Khumbu and Al Read was at his desk in Kathmandu.

From previous trips to the Khumbu and from photographs, we had all hoped that the

**Right** *Loose-heel skiing in the Valley Blanche* (Bill O'Connor).

**Right** *A 'skinny skier' getting in some air time!* (Bill O'Connor).

**Left** *Roskelley on the trek through the Khumbu, near Paugbache, with Ama Dablam beyond* (Bill O'Connor).

**Below** *Peter Hackett gives the thumbs up to the summit team returning to Camp I* (Vern Clevinger).

peak would be climbable, Alpine style, over a few days by a strong party. Looking at the mountain, now for real, it began to reveal its true worth. From quite low down in Himalayan terms, the south-west ridge, the line that we had decided upon, was protected by a great tumbling glacier which was overshadowed by hanging glaciers on the west face. Over the next few days we established a cache of equipment on the spine of a lateral moraine beside the icefall, and whilst John and I did another carry from camp Peter and Vernon had a go at the icefall, hoping to find a route to the ridge. From the top of the moraine we watched them threading a way through the unstable seracs towards the icy headwall which led to the ridge and the col where we hoped to establish our first camp.

Once again we had underestimated it. Back at Base the icefall party returned to the mess tent and huge mugs of tea. 'How was it, you guys?' asked Roskelley, between mouthfuls of peanut-butter-and-jelly-covered biscuits, a delicacy that amongst Americans has equal status with a toasted tea cake or buttered scone! 'Wow, man, it was real freaky,' replied a thoughtful Clevinger. 'Felt as dangerous as the Khumbu icefall. It's not as big, but it's real dangerous' added Hackett, remembering his times through the icefall on his Everest climb from the previous year. We were impressed and asked how far they had got. 'We holed out at a big crevasse, you can't really miss it just follow the wands. We dumped the gear there... it looks as though it might go round to the left,' added Clevinger in slow Californian drawl.

Well before the Himalayan choughs, besides ourselves, had left the nest, Roskelley and I left Base to push the route through the icefall, whilst the others intended carrying another load to our cache camp. The morning as usual had begun quite clear, although before long high cloud was scudding across the sky and forming a pewter-coloured barrier against Cho Oyu at the head of the Ngozumpa valley.

'I'm not sure I like the idea of wandering around the icefall in a white-out.' I said, voicing my fears to John who had already said as much over dinner the night before. He nodded in agreement and kept descending the moraine to the glacier. Once on the ice and lost in play all else was out of mind as well as out of sight! With difficulty we followed the sparse line of bamboo wands that the lads had placed the day before. By the time we reached the end of their trail, cloud had completely filled the cwm and rime was forming on hair and beards. We climbed on, making decisions about the route instinctively, side-stepping and threading our way through the tower block seracs. Then gently, almost unnoticed, the first snows began to fall, a blanket of silence to accompany our blindness. From time to time a snow mass would slide, hissing over the frozen surface, a fearful noise amplified by our tension into massive avalanches that locked us rigid, looking and listening in expectation.

Half-way through the day we crossed a schrund below the headwall leading to a col on the ridge. A second schrund was also crossed where an avalanche had filled it in. Above we waded through steepening granular depth hoar trying to reach a runnel where, hopefully, firmer snow would give climbing to the ridge. John led through fighting for a solid purchase in the steep collapsing granules. 'Keep that rope running' he shouted down as I tried to free it from around a snow mushroom. 'Rope's fixed...come on up'. John had tied the rope off to a snow stake and rested whilst I followed hauling on a jumar.

Climbing the headwall was proving to be all hard work and not enough play. Until then we had been leading through, but 300 ft in the soft deep snow was inefficient and unnecessary. John took over the lead and I carried. About half-way up the slope there was a small rock outcrop and through the swirling mist and spindrift came jerky visions and the muted sounds of him banging in a rock peg. After snow stakes in soft snow the imagined security of the rock was enormous. I have always had this distrust of ice screws, snow stakes and rock pegs, and no matter how they sound when they go in or how good the ice looks, as I put my weight on them I always try to think 'light' and weigh less! But on a security scale of one to ten ice screws always rate higher than snow stakes, and rock pegs come out better followed, I suppose, in this illogical line by natural threads and full weight ropes around the summit blocks of Tryfan!

From the rock band the route ran out left and the play began. Above the snow was fluted and fins of harder ice glistened through. Crossing a runnel we gained a steepening fin and climbed in three superb pitches through a small cornice that led to the col. As I climbed through the cornice John was beaming. 'Wow, man, this is some place.' And it was. The col in

fact turned out to be a sheltered hollow protected on the far side by rocky pinnacles. Despite the weather it looked as though some of the gods were with us. We walked over to the shelter of the pinnacles and threw down our heavy loads. John busied himself making a brew whilst I started levelling a tent platform.

Sitting on our packs enjoying a hot sweet tea the stove spluttered with the job of melting yet more snow. Unknown to us Hackett and Clevinger had given up their rest day and instead of a carry to the cache had carried on. 'Hey, you guys...get a brew on' was the shout that greeted us as Vernon popped his head over the cornice. 'We're coming on through.' In high spirits we photographed Peter on the final pitch of the headwall, jumaring the climbing rope we had left in place. As he pulled over the top we handed him a steaming mug of juice. Tea I might add on this almost all American trip was of the herbal variety under the Celestial Seasonings label!

'Good day's climbing,' said Peter. Then adding as a joke, 'Couldn't let the 'A'-Team go to the top without us.' As we sat on the col

there was a brief clearing and we studied the route above. The south–west ridge led in a sinuous sweep towards the unseen summit. 'If we go for it I reckon we can be up and down in a couple of days,' said John, reflecting the mood of high optimism we were all feeling.

We roped back down the flutings of the headwall leaving ropes in place; we would re-use them to ascend to the col, and pull them up after us.

In the evening Galen arrived at base having trekked up from Phortse. He was bubbling with enthusiasm and happy to be getting on with the climb. He wanted news of everything. The team was together at long last, although Al Read was not going to be able to take part. We sat in the mess-tent on a high with everything set poised. We had planned for the following day to be spent in base getting all of our personal gear straight before 'going for it'. Galen did a carry of his equipment to our cache on the moraine, just for the exercise. He was obviously going well.

The following day was planned as D-day, but it was not to be. Instead the dawn was a miserable affair. Heavy grey cloud filled the valley and a blanket of fresh snow covered the domes. The yaks that grazed around camp were frosted and their warm breath steamed from their mouths forming a rime around their heads. No one had to make the decision to stay in camp, people just didn't bother to get going. Ang Nima and Pemba sensed the mood and prepared favourite foods to satisfy the inner man; great mounds of boiled potatoes, chilli sauce and fried eggs, washed down with gallons of Sherpa ready-made tea, a hot sweet elixir—a mixture of sugar, milk and tea leaves brewed in the same pot, not a hint of celestial seasonings anywhere and like a well-known brand of lager it refreshed parts that even *that* cannot reach!

Three days of foul weather followed our return from the col. Feelings of frustration and gloom etched our optimism and I went down with a dose of giadia, a gut parasite that produces vomiting and Kathmandu quickstep! Feeling very sorry for myself I moped around base, taking everything the good doctor ordered.

Early on the 20th, morning tea brought us from our tents to the first clear sky in days, although to the south huge cumulus castles were boiling up whilst in the deep gorge of the Dudh Kosi a sea of cloud lapped against the hillside of rhododendron. With light loads we set off towards cache camp with Ang Nima burning juniper and moaning a toneless mantra for our safety.

Our dump of gear on the moraine was under a mantle of snow which we cleared finding our double boots and one piece suits. Geared and loaded up we sped down the now familiar side of the moraine on to the glacier. Familiarity bred no contempt, the dangers had not changed and Peter reminded us, 'Just like the Khumbu...not as big...but we have got the west face'. As we roped up, a big serac above and to the left broke away and crashed down the face disintegrating into particles and covering the upper glacier with a cloud of ice dust which billowed towards us and then as if consumed disappeared like a spectre without trace.

Better acclimatized now, the route through the commando course of the icefall went quickly. The bamboo wands marking the route passed by like the bell at the end of each round in a title fight; ten down...five to go...seconds out..ding! Fearing the consequences of what an avalanche would mean, but wanting more of what turning back would deny does not leave any options. My journal recalls:

> Real pleasure today. Felt totally committed to the climb; nothing else mattered. Same kind of adrenalin high I get on rock at home when climbing is all that matters, not protection, not how difficult or small the holds are, just wanting to do the next move and to be there climbing.

At the col we savoured the day's efforts. Whilst John and Galen put up the other tents, the three of us had a look at the ridge ahead, intending to leave our climbing ropes fixed on it to give us a good start in the morning. Almost at once the reality of the ridge was appreciated. Instead of giving straightforward climbing on steep neve, the surface turned out to be brittle ice and the ridge itself sculptured into strange mushrooms of an unstable geometry hidden from below. The climbing was very insecure indeed. Forced to climb out right around an overhanging split in the ridge the truth of its difficulty dawned. At the end of the third pitch we tied off the rope to an ice screw and rappelled in a direct line back to the col.

We sat outside the tents enjoying the last of the day's warmth. It was a spectacular sunset of disturbing colours and ever changing light through a mass of clouds. All the talk was silenced as we watched the dying day. Still fighting the giardia I nursed a slight headache and a need to throw up!

The freeze-dried food, despite the promise of the packet, looked grim as it congealed to the plastic mug that served as plate and cup. These Americans have such different standards! Liquid held more appeal; I drank and chewed a couple of diamox. As ever before a big climb sleep was fitful. I have always envied those that could sleep through anything. All I was aware of was tomorrow and snow hissing over the nylon of the tents. At 3.30 am digital bleeps shocked us into reality and the noise of the MSR stoves was as intrusive as trail-bikes on the Marlborough Downs. Peter had had a rough night. Unable to sleep and breath properly, he, the doctor, diagnosed flu.

We were faced with a crisis. If we waited a day or two we would have to go down to restock and the daily pre-monsoon storms with their afternoon snow seemed to be building into something big. It was a difficult decision. Peter had put the trip together. He was the catalyst for our group and now we were to deny him the chance of going to the top.

The decision made, it is time to go. Despite the fact that everything had been cut to a minimum the packs seem huge. As ever safety and survival depend on an optimal amount of gear. We are cutting it fine. It is decided that whoever is out front will be lightly loaded, letting them move as quickly and as safely as possible. The others will follow using a jumar on the fixed climbing rope thus giving the leader a chance to rest and recover. The last man will take out all the gear and pass it on. From the high point of the previous evening five very steep ice pitches follow. Roskelley who is outfront shouts down, 'We've got to get rid of these loads. We'll never make it at this rate.' The screw was turning and the last 'virgin' in the Khumbu was letting us know why she was so.

The climbing is steep and technical on ice that varies from hard blue-green stuff to a kind of atmospheric soufflé! At around 19,500 ft after climbing over a series of rocky pinnacles there is a slight dip in the ridge where we cut a platform for our two small tents. Whilst Clevinger and I hack away at the platform, Rowell and Roskelley push upwards to give us a two pitch flyer in the morning. Shattered from navvying we watch them as John leads, climbing around bulges and traversing rightwards over a massive drop beneath a line of overhangs built from a curling snow crest. They rapell back down shouting for a brew! We spend the rest of the day rehydrating; an almost impossible task at this altitude.

'It should go but it's hard', said John. 'We won't be able to climb along the ridge. Gonna have to climb beneath it and try the diagonal ramp above the huge buttresses of the south face. Really scary, if you come off... you're out over the overhangs,' he said dryly.

Three thirty and more digital bleeps. Robot-like I pull on clothing before leaving the cocoon. Supping tepid squash helps to suppress nausea before the hassle with double boots and then out for the off. Cold and immobile the haul up the first rope with a frozen jumar is a nightmare of incompetent movement and fumbling. Ice screws won't clear, glasses keep steaming up and moving around bulges doing off-balance moves scares the hell out of me. By the end of the third

pitch commitment and rhythm surge back and the day's light gives a new perspective to the route ahead.

Roskelley, climbing confidently and fast, dances sideways up the steepening ramp. Crouching below an overhang he lays away off his axe planted in an icicle and gains an upward step. Perhaps 15 or 20 rope lengths later the way ahead is barred by a huge serac barrier forming a step in the ridge which is split by a massive crevasse. From a rocky perch, a platform jutting from the ice, the route leads up and leftwards into the back of a rift and so onto the face of the serac. Two more long pitches up seemingly vertical ice lead to the shoulder of the cliff. For the first time since morning we perch together. We are all surprised by the difficulty. The clouds billow in and it begins to snow lightly.

Apart from our climbing gear we decide to leave the sacks on the serac. In the white-out I lead off and quickly come to a halt. At the far side of the serac is another monster crevasse leaving our block detached from the main ridge. We spread out and it is Roskelley crawling rightward who finds a sliver of ice arching across the gap. Lying flat he crocodiles across and climbs a vertical step on the far side. We have gained the summit plateau. The visibility is almost zero and a squall flurries the snow about. A great bergschrund is bridged where it butts against yet another vertical ice wall. Searching for a weakness we traverse left until passing time forces a decision and a direct line up bulging ice leads to a weakness in the wall where a gash like a sabre cut splits the ridge ahead and slices down the face offering a sheltered stance. From this hollow a wavy wall of ice leads to the ridge above dividing the south and west facets of the mountain. Now on the ridge we are reduced to the horizontal by a section of depth hoar that falls to a length of schoolboy dog-paddle! For a brief moment there is a clearing in the clouds and ahead we can see the summit a few rope lengths away. Like prostrate pilgrims before the mountain we caterpillar forwards until a final steep pitch of climbing leads to a section of ridge curving to the summit.

Finally, exposed to the full fury of the wind and snow we edge along the crest until one at a time we stand on the summit of Cholatse. Winners of a summit, losers of a dream.

But that was only half the game.

With axes buzzing and scalps tingling we

*Leaving the bivouac at 21,000 ft on Cholatse. Behind Taweche shows through the cloud* (Bill O'Connor).

lingered, briefly relishing our summit. Gripped about the building storm and the fact that our sacks were on the serac below we hurriedly roped down the ice wall to our 'life-support' packs. Far too late to get down to camp we were faced with a bivouac on the open plateau on top of the serac! With no energy or enthusiasm for hole building, each withdrew into the solitary confinement of his pit. During the night the storm blew itself out but not before the snow had insiduously found its way into our tightly drawn sleeping bags. Between clenched teeth shivering thoughts were fixed on descent. As I said before I hate rapping off ice screws and like a child, I found myself wishing I could be transported back to base with its luxury and security without having to go through the ordeal of the descent. But then what are the nights for if it is not for dreaming?

Dawn was a watery affair. The storm had passed but the sky was still confused with layers of cloud. One by one we managed to pick out the peaks of Everest, Makalu, Cho Oyu, Nuptse and Chomolhari in Tibet as the sun struck them.

The 20 or so abseils, many of them swinging sideways along the ramp, were filled with high tension. Each of us was fearful of the abyss below the ramp where a slip would mean a swing into space. By the time we reached our high camp the thin, cold air and fear had left us parched. Camp provided a respite and a chance to brew and pack our things before the final airy flight down to Hackett whom we had left at the col. Already a day overdue we knew he would be worried and hungry, as we had taken most of the food! Unknown to us those at base camp had seen us for a brief moment just below the summit. Not knowing that Peter had stayed behind they had counted only four and imagined the worst. By the time we reached Peter it was snowing again. Unable to fully hide his disappointment he congratulated us and pushed around some hot liquid. The cupboard was bare! We packed up camp and cleared the site, leaving nothing on the mountain, and then ran the gauntlet of the icefall for the last time. With total relief we gained the moraine and wandered slightly apart down the valley towards base, to be met by Al

Read and our Sardar who handed out flasks of hot orange. Everyone was full of the joys of spring. But then that's when a young man's fancy turns to...the alps and ski-touring.

A marvellous alternative to tropical sun is the high Alps in May. Gone are most of the hoards; now, only the devotees of touring are on the slopes above 'the slopes' to search out the spring corn, fabulous granular skiing snow, kind to mistakes and making the most daunting off-piste slope possible. But that's on a good day and they are the ones we want to remember, not the heavy mashed potatoes snow that was all the reward for a hard climb to a col or the ever breaking crust that plays cat and mouse with your skis.

Wanting my cake and eating it, which has always seemed perfectly natural to me, I spent April in Nepal and returned to Heathrow just in time to fly to Geneva. This not because of any desperate urge to keep going, but through an administrative screw up on my part.

In fact it was really Gillettes fault; not the shaver, but the skier, Ned Gillette. It was his enthusiasm for three-pin downhill touring and love of adventure that fired me to have a go and to try to overcome my prejudice of skinny skis. Along with much of the skiing fraternity I had relegated them to the overweight shuffling brigade seen spotty dogging around the edges of resorts or as the preserve of cardio-respiratory freaks in search of oxygen debt. As far as my own love, ski mountaineering, was concerned, no way! But, as I said, Gillette, along with advances in equipment, changed all that.

The theory is this: with good metal edged telemark ski and a suitable three-pin binding a reasonable downhill skier should be able to transfer his skills to loose-heel skiing. Combine this with a desire for the ultimate aesthetic thrill – a series of linked telemarks, and you are half-way there. In practice of course what the reasonably competent downhiller has to face up to is looking a complete wally as he tumbles about on the piste and kick-turns down the easiest of mogul fields whilst executing what Gillette aptly calls the 'flying-buttocks arrest' as he or she continues to search for the most aesthetic thrill in skiing! For those that persist on the piste the reward will be nirvana.

But back to the Alps in May. On my return from Nepal I fleet-footed it to Arolla, that gem of an Alpine village in the Valais. Ready and waiting were a bunch of friends from the London Regional Nordic Ski Club all devotees of the long thin ski, and above all happy to be in the mountains. Our aim was simple, to search for nirvana in the form of spring corn and telemarks on that section of the Haute Route between Arolla and Zermatt, and to throw in a couple of peaks on the way.

Arolla was as friendly as ever and although there was hardly a tourist about they kept the lifts running so that we could have a day, wallying about, on the piste. I am not a Freudian, but the pleasure-pain principle seems particularly applicable to telemarking. Without doubt all of us gained a great deal of pleasure from that day of turns and tumbles and the lunging, swooping arcs of the telemarks we carved. But the next morning as we skinned to the Pas d'Chevre en-route for the Cabin Dix some of us experienced the pain born of that pleasure!

The Dix was full. What could one expect; the weather was typically May with a full, blue sky and wonderfully warm, and the snow. Of such things are dreams made of. Most of the others at the hut were Swiss and local, although a few were French and had begun their 'tour' in Chamonix. I must say I enjoy Alpine hut life. Having sat on the terrace soaking-up last of the sun, the hut with its bustle is an amazing contrast to the world of rock and ice outside. But a satisfying meal and a bottle of wine in good company having spent a day doing what you enjoy most must be close to the elusive nirvana.

The morning of course is not a good time for skiers but for the skinny skier pre-dawn starts after a cold clear night are a particular kind of hell. The surface outside the hut was corrugated ice and the slope leading to the glacier steep. It is at this point that romance gives way to mechanics and the skinny skier is at his greatest disadvantage. It is also the time when there are the maximum number of other skiers about to see you 'wallying' and so reinforce their belief that nordic skis should be confined to the valley. Once on the glacier of course all was resolved and the light boots and skis with the greater freedom of the binding make uphill skiing a pleasure. Apart from a few slipping problems, the result of a very narrow skin remedied by the age old trick of a bit of cord wrapped around the ski, the climb to the Col de la Serpentine went well and we enjoyed a marvellous sunrise over the Dent Blanche

and Matterhorn.

The day remained clear and warm and from the summit of the Pigne d'Arolla, surely one of the finest viewpoints in the Alps, we looked out over the peaks of the Pennines, Oberland, Grand Paradiso, Mt Blanc and Dauphine massives. With our skis upended in the snow a little below the summit we munched on Emmental and chocolate, Switzerland's contribution, along with the cuckoo clock, to Western civilization. We dallied, as satisfied folk are apt to do, before the descent to the Vignettes.

Looking back, dallying could have been our undoing. Going up we had looked fine; every inch a group of well honed skinny ski mountain tourers, strong of arm and thick of leg! But those extra moments spent lingering before the run down have been the downfall of many a tourer. From the summit to the Col du Brenay the snow was perfect, granular and accommodating, with enough on the surface for well-carved turns and to throw some sparkle against the sun as well as to cushion the ever so infrequent fall! And for a while, at least, after the col, the snow held up. But then...

The explanation of course is simple. The Vignettes side of the Pigne catches the first of the sun as it rises above the horizon over the Dent Blanche, whilst we were skinning up the sunless side from the Dix. Now the metamorphosis had occurred and what an hour before would have been pure joy was pure purgatory that increased with every foot descended. The top few inches that once was corn was now like a thick school porridge that

grabbed at your skis making them run in a quick, quick, slow motion, throwing you forward and sitting you back. The head plant and flying buttocks arrest on these occasions becomes the norm and as I looked back up the steep, heavy slope leading to the Col Chermontane it looked as though some cataclysm had occurred. Indeed it had as members of the LRNSC dived, rolled and somersaulted their descent. At various times there were legs and skis kicking the air, whilst heads, ostrich-like, were planted in the snow. Others, fearing all was lost, bailed out, while some, perhaps the result of schooling and a frozen upper lip, accelerated towards the inevitable massive tumble bringing forth cheers from their peers. Without doubt all part of the pleasure/pain principle!

At the foot of the slope we re-grouped and in good order entered the haven of the Vignettes Hut. Battered but not beaten! Bravo! I think is what the locals said. What Jean and Elizabette the guardians said is not suitable for print, but then he is an old friend and not typically Swiss in his reserve!

The following morning we were away early, long before dawn, in an attempt to be well on our way to Zermatt before the sun had done desperate things to the snow on the marvellous run from the top of the Tete Valpalline via the Stockje and the Zmutt Glacier to Zermatt. But as they say, it is a long way between cup and lip, and certainly there was many a slip *en route*. It was not really dark as we left the hut and traversed under the seracs of the Pigne. A nasty little jump over a small schrund had us flying — and I do mean flying — on towards

the Petit Mt Collon. Up over the Oetemma Glacier a veil of cloud heralded poor weather from Italy and high cirrus upheld the promise. By the time we made the Col L'Eveque it was snowing, although the cloud was light and visibility was good. On the far side of the col the run was perfect until an icy stretch through a steep crevassed section had us 'doing our thing'. As we schussed towards the Bouquetins in fine style, several other parties cut short their tour heading down the glacier back to Arolla. But the day was young and armed with map, compass and altimeter we poled onwards and upwards towards the Col du Mt Brule. The slope was surprisingly steep and icy, and had a definite convex feel to it, and those new to the alpine skinning game found the radical kick turns at the end of each traverse trying. By now the Matterhorn had a grey lenticular cap whilst westwards streaks and streamers of cloud were filling in the spaces between the peaks and the colour was gone from the picture.

It's an ill wind, as they say. The snow on the descending traverse to the Haute Glacier de Tsa de Tsan was spot on, exactly what we had been searching for even if we had to schuss over its surface in complete white out and falling snow. By the time gravity pulled us to a halt, it was time to put the skins on again. I always think it is one of the strangest sensations when you ski through thick cloud and the slope merges without trace into it. There's no sensation of speed just an awareness of movement. Often the only time I know I have stopped is when I fall over because I leaned away from or into an

imagined slope!

By now the race was on to get to the Col Valpelline before the sun had done for the descent and we were once again hacking our way through crud. Now was the time for the cardio-vascular freaks to set a pace more akin to a Vassoloppet racers than classical ski mountaineers. Once at the col everyone had enjoyed the effort. Again the old 'P and P' syndrome was at work! Our decision to press on had also been rewarded with the ill wind blowing us some good in the form of cooler weather for the climb. Not only that the cloud had kept the sun off the snow which was now set fair for our triumphant descent into Zermatt.

For my money, this run ranks with the best in ski mountaineering. To begin with it is over 12 km long, which for many downhill only types would be a good day's skiing, yet here it is simply the icing on the Haute Route cake. In terms of scenery it is one of the grandest spots in the Alps. As you ski through a maze of massive crevasses towards the Stockje, a rock island in a sea of ice, you are surrounded by alpine four thousanders like the Dent Blanche, Dent d'Herens, Matterhorn and Ober Gablehorn. Yet the skiing is good with intricate navigation through crevasse systems, often open, whilst later a wide, open couloir ends with a steep traverse under seracs and the rocks of the Stockje. You are always aware of the possible danger of hidden crevasses, for it is true to say that on the High Level Route good mountaineering skills are often in greater demand than skiing skills. In poor weather the route finding can be difficult in this area, but

*Skinning to a high col caught by the sunlight on the Haute Route* (Bill O'Connor).

today the heralds were false and the sky had gradually cleared with only high, thin clouds to veil the sun.

Once on the Zmutt glacier we traversed down its true right bank. The snow was holding up although the rocks were showing through and we hurried to be away from possible rock and ice avalanches, always a danger, from the hanging Matterhorn glacier, below the north face. Before Furi we joined the ski slopes below Stafel Alp. Summer felt just around the corner. At a traditional wooden hay loft, converted, thankfully, into a beer cellar we drank to a great day's skiing, to telemarking, to the Haute Route...to absent friends...to the friends of absent friends and even their friends — and I'm sure if we had the money and the beer not run out we would have lifted our glasses to you and your friends! But the call of Zermatt was heard, albeit faintly. So we rallied and shouldered our skis to wander through meadows of waining snow and pink-headed crocus and the occasional soldanella, true signs that summer's season is at hand and it is time to sharpen ice axe and crampons and dream of summer climbing in the alps. For that's where a mountaineer's fancy turns...

Bill O'Connor is Managing Director of O'Connor Adventure UK, a trekking and expedition company that run trips to the Himalayas, the Karakoram, the Alps and to Africa. Bill is one of Britain's leading Himalayan expeditioners and has several first ascents of Himalayan peaks to his credit.

A noted wilderness photographer, Bill O'Connor's work has been promoted by Nikon and has been published in all of Britain's outdoor magazines. A former head of outdoor education at Marlborough College, Bill has also worked with Peter Livesey at Bingley College of Education and he now lives in Harrogate in Yorkshire with his wife Sally.

# *June: British Rock*

## TERRY GIFFORD

> For in June there's a red rose bud
> And that's the flower for me
> But often I have snatched at that red rose
>   bud
> And gained the willow tree
> And gained the willow tree.

The first of June usually occurs unnoticed towards the end of a Whitsun holiday during which I have already been climbing a fair bit. When I look at the list of routes I have climbed on the first of June I find that they are some of my most warmly evocative climbs — high points projecting from a rich texture of memories like the flora of the approach to a crag; Glen Etive's fistfuls of pink and purple rhododendrons, the knee-deep heather crossed to the cliffs of The Island and the textures of various clumps dressing the limestone at Gogarth. At the end of June comes my birthday and a new style of party I have adopted. But let's begin at the beginning of the month.

As I write this it is raining and it is June. What is assumed to be the month of hottest sun and the longest days can produce severe frustration, as the peak of fitness wastes away whilst watching slabs steaming after days of heavy rain. That is how it was one year when we were camping in Glen Etive for a week at Whitsun. Tim Noble had been very good about it really, thinking that there would be just me and him, but finding that we had to pick up the photograper on the way. He had wondered why I had put my tent in beside his when he had called for me. The photographer had never camped before, so she found our week beside the loch under the Etive slabs packed with exciting new experiences. There was a first experience of the Scottish midge, breakfasting on the breakfast eater. There was the problem of avoiding Tim taking a shower in the waterfall above the bridge. There was also a dramatic first discovery of the Highland sheep tick and its delightful habit of seeking out the darkest folds of the human body.

It rained for three days non-stop. One day, in sheer frustration, we took a wine-box up Glen Nevis and sat in the car warming our insides and burning the backs of our throats on what Tim characterized in a mock Cockney accent as 'Roogemont Carsil, a great little British wine'. Then, in a suitably insane state we pulled on rock-boots and padded through boggy grass to climb on Polldubh in the rain. The wet slap of slippery rock always brings you round from these intoxicating ideas. But at least we came down to earth having done a route, and it was in the spirit of things that it was called 'Heatwave'. Back in Fort William, we found ourselves warming up again with a curry in a room full of sooty-faced eighteenth-century Campbells, plus a few uniformed dragoons, hungry from a full day's filming of 'The Highlander'. Down by Loch Etive again, we hung our harnesses of gear to dry from the solitary tree beside our camp and, as the weather improved, replaced them with another wine-box.

One day it stopped raining for a bit and we went off to wade across the waterfalls running down the Etive slabs, finding that the friction works even when there is not an inch of dry rock on Spartan Slab. I could not believe that it would go. I remember at one point putting a toe in a little Etive scoop of a hold and watching the water run over my boot-end. My head told me this was unlikely to stick, but this was my first experience of the sparkling Etive granules of granite, and to my surprise it stuck. (Rab Carrington has since told me it is a well-known fact that Spartan Slab is a route that actually has *holds*.) We pulled over the overlap half-way up, traversed the thin line above, only to be caught by a man-eating wall of rain rising up the Loch from the sea. I sacrificed two prussik loops for the abseil and we bounced down the ropes, soaked to the skin yet again.

As the week improved we went round the East Face of Aonach Dubh to paddle up to a Weeping Wall before singing our way up Archer Ridge by the galloping direct finish.

Setting out for Rannoch Wall, one finally cloudless day, we choked on the smoke blowing across the moor and risked being overrun by the battle being fought at the top of the Pass of Glencoe. Standards and kilts fluttered behind us, horses and film-crew neighed down the wind, whilst rifles and film-directors exploded loudly for yet another take of gulping abseil which reached the ground only with rope-stretch. At the top of the secure bridging up Agag's Groove my stomach fluttered as Tim directed that we abseil off a block, but no amount of neighing from me would deter him. After we had ascended the steepening Red Slab there had to be, of course, another take of that gulping abseil which reached the ground only with rope-stretch. The photographer clicked away from a perch on Curved Ridge.

Well away from the Glencoe media circus, our quiet evenings were passed round Tim's Himalayan fire, with sorties to the wine-tree, whilst owls echoed across Glen Etive.

The last day of our week together was a climax of blue sky, glistening white rock, and at last, ascents of Spartan Slab and Hammer. The photographer, sunbathing all day on the coffin-block below, became a scantily-clad siren of the slabs whom everyone had to pause and consult, conferring on her the authority of instant expert. I swung into the lead on the first three pitches of Spartan Slab, confidence artificially high now that the rock was dry. At first attempt I found that the trick of the overlap was to push down and mantleshelf, rather than over-reach and snatch at the jug so that pedalling feet lost contact with the finest friction in Britain. Beware the snatch and pull. After that I knew the 25 ft hand traverse would bite a small friend. But I hadn't led the crux, and a descending traverse rightwards still caught my breath as my head resisted the messages from my feet. I was glad Tim had taken over for the second half of what is actually the easiest route on the slab.

Hammer is thinner and harder, more of a head-banger. Here I really discovered that the secret of Etive slab-crabbing is to keep moving just enough to maintain a little communication gap between the feet and the head. At a sort of scoop, for example, which gives access to the lovely long line of the slab's corner, there are no second goes. Once you start padding up, the fingers become frictioning feet reading the slightest indentation in the glaring white surface of the glasspaper. The corner itself keeps opening and closing as a layback becomes necessarily more walking up than laying back. Once again a traverse became my crux, despite Tim's being belayed above in the nest of overhangs. The absorbing wandering through the final little slabs concluded a thousand feet of climbing on the great slide of slabs that had dominated our camp and a magical week deep in the arms of Glen Etive. When we broke out of the glen for the last time, we knew that something special had been left behind and yet something of it would stay with us.

---

*The glaring white glasspaper of the Etive Slabs* (Gill Round).

### Etive Time

On the third day of rain
Their watches stopped.
Glen Etive time took hold
Of their heads, the way light,
Surreal, red, inside the tent
Seemed to penetrate their brains,
The way the rain drumming
Its mantra on the taut,
Thin, red skin so close
To their eardrums on the ground
Beat the retreat to uneasy sleep.

On the fourth day, although rain stopped
Actually falling as if for the Flood
The sky of mist pressed down
On their prone bodies, a grey weight
Level as the loch, its heavy mirror
Two hundred feet above the slow,
Slow tides. Etive time still held.

On the fifth day a wine-box
Hung from the tree at evening.
Pine-scented smoke rolled from a circle
Of white quartz stones. Heads lifted
To the glen-echoing owl
And midges made forays behind
The ears. Etive time unwound.

On the sixth day breakfast
Pacing the road already burning,
Sweat sweet for bites to the head,
Too light, too hot, too early,
Awaiting the start for the slabs
Surely a source of thermal movement
In the great stone clock of Etive time.

On the seventh day the serpent rested
In Glen Etive under the purple blooms
Of rhododendrons in abandon
As their small white car wound up
Against the rhythm of the river still
Cutting and shaping, feeding and taking,
In the watered clock of rock.
Their lives now sprung from Etive time.

For nearly ten successive Whitsuns I had been going to The Island off the west coast of Scotland. Here the first of June would catch me crossing ankle-turning tussocks of grass. Beyond deep heather there is a sea-cliff that you will not find in any guidebook. Traversing around the front of one buttress on my last visit, I looked across a gully to the next seaward-facing buttress. A dark old eagle lifted off and soared round the corner, returning for just one last look at the intruder. A peregrine screamed out, climbed high in the sky and fell past me, still crying with shrill intensity. I watched a raven return to its huge twiggy nest under an overhang and then I traversed back above the sea, testing each granite flake and eyeing unclimbed lines through the unknown rock above.

Now you will understand why I prefer to call this place just The Island. It does not hide some fabulous crag, it is not the last great wilderness, and it is just as fragile as many unpublicized corners of the Highland and Islands. We really ought to leave some areas of rock unguided if the opportunity for wilderness climbing is to be there for those who come to seek it out. Some sea-cliffs should be left, too, for the eagle, peregrine and raven to share, without any more than occasional and accidental disturbance from the climber. Soon there may even be a glimpse of the sea-eagle eyeing up these cliffs for itself, as they reach breeding age after their successive years of being released from the reintroduction programme on Rhum.

Pete, the only climber on The Island, is an English incomer whose children have all been born and grown up here in this Gaelic culture. He has spent years systematically traversing round the rocks of the coastline and there are few sections between bays that he has been unable to cross. For a few years on and off he has found a climbing partner on the island, a teacher or a lighthousekeeper, before they moved on to other postings and other islands. Currently he is climbing with the doctor who goes out with him on sunny evenings to a little craggy headland between two long white strands. Here they boulder when they are not exploring new routes at easy grades in the steep-sided gullies that slope to the sea, or on the odd slab across a cliff, or on the little stacks that can decorate the end of a beach. It was on just such a beach that Norman made a new route for Pete's personal notebook of climbs.

When our children were little and we took them across the moor to look down on this particular bay that is enclosed by steep grass and rocky headlands, they named this The Wooden Beach. It appeared to be almost covered with driftwood, some of it the size of the largest planks they had ever seen. They searched amongst flotsam for hours whilst Andy and I found a way out on to the left headland and climbed its spine for two pitches of V Diff to reach the 'dun' indicated on the map at its highest point. Here an Iron Age fort is still visible as an undisturbed circular wall which has remained perched on the ridge in windy isolation looking down on The Wooden Beach.

A weaker, parallel ridge of rock projecting across the beach has been broken into a series of small stacks, a seaward one having been split like the eye of a needle. One year Norman, having already failed on this steep little stack, turned his attention to a groove in the 90 ft wall of rock that abuts the back of the bay. He set about decorating it with his nuts. (This was before Norman had any friends.) Slowly bridging and jamming, in his steady, well-protected style, he led to the top of the small wall. Eventually Pete, Andy and I stood beside him looking out across the beach.

It is a strange, primitive ritual, this desire to stand on top of a rockface and look out quietly. Around us the fulmars wheeled and red deer peered cautiously over the cliff. Unseen otters were scent-marking their patch amongst boulders and caves. Standing a mere 60 ft above the busy, empty beach there was no way we were given any power over this place. Yet we too had marked our territory in our heads, achieved an odd perspective on it all by exploring a little upright rock, marked ourselves off from most of our species in an absurdly meaningless way. What we did not know that year was that high within the eye of the needle there lived the black, red-beaked chough, incubating the mysterious knowledge of its cave-loving kind.

At the other end of Britain, June swells into a different kind of fullness. The green-banked lanes that lead towards Land's End reach out their grasses and their flowers towards the incoming cars. Four of us were crammed into a Mini for this trip from Sheffield on several successive years in the late '60s. All spare air space in the car was filled with rucksacks of climbing and camping gear, based on the assumption that once neatly packed in, bodies did not need to move. If they did, this was considered some form of anti-social self-indulgence. In several over-loaded and under-powered small cars the remnants of the college climbing club met up, give or take a day for 'blowing up on the motorway', at the wonderfully named Rosemergy Farm, within sight of the top pitches of Bosigran Main Cliff.

The Peter Biven guide was new, the days were long, the rock was warm and the cider was an education. Whillans-style flat-caps were *de rigueur* at the time and I found one left behind in the Tinner's Arms at Zennor. I also took to climbing in a fisherman's smock, finding it an ideal, simple wind-proof garment in which I continue to climb. I remember a dominant spirit of unbounded enthusiasm, for the cliffs which we explored with the warmest of wonder and for the pubs which we explored for the most dangerous of drinks. It was what the Alpine Club calls 'a mixed party' and we were in love in Cornwall in June.

But my relationship with climbing at that time was not so simple. I was fascinated and intimidated in equal proportions, which meant that I found myself waking up in the mornings to a complex mixture of emotions. I savoured the excitement and the aesthetics, but shrank from the descents and the difficulties. After getting to the bottom of Ash Can Gully at Chair Ladder I was a wreck and Jock McKinney's hair-raising description of Flannel Avenue as 'steep, exposed and dominated by a black pool winking up at you between your toes' certainly had the desired effect. I still haven't done it. Watching Dave Harbour lean out horizontally it seemed, clutching the great 'bull's testicle' that hangs above Demo Route, scared me out of another straight Severe.

But climbing with Norman on Doorpost, at the seaward side of Bosigran's big face visible from our campsite, was an intimidation gratefully to be overcome. The step out of the shelter of the sentry-box to start the twin cracks of the second pitch suddenly gave the sense of seriousness which demands that the holds of the rock be read in the right order, rather than snatched at desperately. I remember that the moment of mental steadying was vibrant with a little of the old leg-shake.

It was Pete Biven's holiday guidebook that first alerted me to Lawrence's connection with Cornwall and first drew me to Zennor where Lawrence had stayed. After a recent visit and a reaquaintance with the Zennor mermaid that was carved under a seat in the church by a Saxon craftsman I went on, later the same day, to climb with Tim and John Baker on a crag which was unclimbed during my first visits to Cornwall. Carn Kenidjack holds a route called Saxon that is again both intimidating and fascinating as unseen holds appear in a sheer wall to render a HVS lead a full rope length of absorbing moves that are only VS.

Perhaps this paradox of intimidation and fascination reflects the quality of Cornwall itself, its bright, beautifully-textured surfaces containing a darker undertow of sea and legend and earlier, other knowledge. This is the spirit of the Zennor mermaid and, for me, it is the spirit of the cliff-climbing too.

### Saxon Mermaid

I entered Zennor church uneasily,
Curiosity fighting childhood sermon
   memories
Mingled with this sense I'd rationally
   dismiss
Of submitting once again to an upright
   tower,
These foresquare stones, the judgement
Of this dark door whose latch I choose to
   lift.

But I stepped into a granite cave of light
   where
Columns and arches glinted pink and
   white.
On them rested the familiar form of an
   upturned
Boat in the roof of barrel vaulting. Spring
   flowers
Led us in our search for the pagan image
Carved in wood disguised as a seat.

She is hard and dark, the Zennor mermaid,
Defaced by someone's fear of her eyes,
But the swell of her hips, the swirl of grain
In her navel, its centred depths, and her
   salty
Low-slung tail of scales still tell what
   tempted
The chorister down to Pendour Cove to
   enter sea.

And later that same day I abseiled into a
   zawn
To stand before a climb called 'Saxon',
   nervous
Below that towering slab, brittle, steep and
   black.
Two attempts to unlock its start, then
   glancing back
There you were, curled on the flowered
   headland,
Waving, smiling, bright as the Cornish
   light.

Somehow spectacular abseils are a feature of climbing with Tim. Rain may have forced us to abseil down the Etive Slabs but perversity had led us down the Rannoch Wall. And, perversely, the abseil down the side of Saxon following the line of Gneiss Gnome was Tim's way of avoiding a perfectly gneiss scramble down to sea-level. In Anglesey too, at the top of Dream of White Horses Tim sought out the lowest possible block at the top of Wen Slab so that to swing from a ledge on to the abseil rope was to find yourself immediately in space 300 ft above the sea. I must admit that the thought of the two abseils we were about to make was rather blinkered by awareness of the profusion of June flowers that Gill was photographing around the top of the cliff. We had escaped a wet day in the Llanberis Pass to find that Angelsey's North Stack was dry and bright. A dream was about to be fulfilled.

When I first came here to climb Dream with David Craig and the original Dreamer, Ed Drummond, it was the last day of December and water was cascading down the slab. It was not difficult to bow out and allow David to follow Ed across the main pitch to escape up Wen just before dark. When Tim last came here he had abseiled off the end of the rope into the sea. A big wave had lifted him up so that he could make a grab for the end of the rope which had sprung back up the wall. Now, at low tide on a calm day, Tim, John and I gathered in good order on the black platform that is cut into the bottom right-hand corner of this vast white slab.

The first pitch is really not to be missed if the tide is low and white horses are confined to dreams. A long pitch climbs the lower wall, on limestone which requires a little tuning into, as you decide how best to use the interesting variety of rounded cracks and flutings. The steepness prevents this from becoming an exercise in aesthetics and an awareness of the 500 ft of VS climbing ahead encourages an economy of movement and balance. When we had gathered together at the little ledge below the notch, John set off on the famous traverse, his multi-coloured Joseph jumper and ski-hat necessary even in June.

The line of finger holds here is quite positive and although it gets thinner further away from the belay and a deft change of feet may be necessary, it is a mistake to regard this as the crux, in my view. The climb is beautifully evenly balanced in that every pitch feels 4C.

Thinking that the crux is over at the end of the second pitch could be a mistake. By the time all three of us had crossed into the crackline of Wen, we were suspended for a while between each other's legs in a stack of three hanging belays like parachutists without chutes. Tim's cigar smoke drifted up between our legs.

Each pitch is also unique in character on this climb, as might be expected from a climb which was assembled in parts, only pitches two and three having been climbed on the first ascent. Pitch three is odd and awkward. A crack curves steeply away up to the left and its bottom edge is rounded but textured by tiny flakes of limestone. I found myself frictioning with the left half of my body and jamming with the right, trying to ascend diagonally upwards. Security felt partial; balance seemed rotational; concentration was total.

If pitches two and three are traverse lines following natural breaks in the rock, the final pitch of Dream of White Horses brings into play the verb 'to traverse'. This is the ability to find a line by the repeated process of 'looking round the corner to see where it might go'. Although it might be said that this final pitch follows a slab between two overhangs, it is more accurate to describe it as crossing a fan of folded yellow paper. It needs handling gently as the tops of some of the edges, from which one is tempted to lower oneself, want to become crumpled. The key question to be answered in performing this traversing act is where to go up and where to step down. Thus is this traverse 'made' rather than 'followed', for a full lonely length of the rope. Out at the top of the cliff it was June again. Seapinks sprang out of their green cushions, and out of the white rocks all around yellows and whites splashed amongst clumps of ochre and rich greens.

When June comes to Derbyshire climbers come up out of the towns after work to stretch their stems of rope up the rock, spread the leaves of their hands across the gritstone and raise their heads above the edges towards the evening sky. They start out in shorts and end up shivering in the breeze, belaying on the edge of night. Each year at this time, I make a return to Rivelin Edge after having left it to lie at the back of my mind all winter, green and lichenous. Each year at this time, I set off in shorts and each year I forget how high and thick the nettles get in June. The best salve, after the dock leaves that fortunately flourish

*Climber Norman Elliott stands triumphant on Rivelin Needle* (Terry Gifford).

beside the nettles, is to do Face Climb No 1 solo behind Rivelin Needle. Sharp edges tempt you up the steepening slab until you find that it is really a wall with a long reach for the top edge. The fingers fold into its dip as soon as they close over the top. Then it is a trot along to Wilkinson Wall to do it again at a harder grade, 20 ft of Hard Severe, building on the confidence of a comfortable V Diff.

That symbolizes the pattern of my climbing on the edges during warm June evenings and sweaty, sociable Saturdays. At Millstone, for example, I find that I can solo Lambeth Chimney (Hard Severe) then second something at HVS, although often not without a struggle. (It is the way Norman makes sure his runners always stay in that gives me such epics getting them out.) Looking back, I find that it was during this month that I struggled up some of the hardest climbs I've done at Millstone. I remember being weighted like a diver by a waist belt strung with big nuts, as I lay-backed up the final section of Estremo. The delicate direct start to Lyons Corner House, by contrast, I remember as pure delight when I was led up it by a pupil after school one evening.

This year was to be the year of Great Portland Street, my first HVS lead. Well, let me admit straight away that it was not really, before Majorie Allen and Mike Mortimer tell you that their dog saw me pull on a runner halfway up the groove. That's if they didn't see the goings on at the start as well.

You see, Norman and I have this helpful little ritual that we have established over the years whereby, whilst the leader is tying on, the second solos up the start of the route a bit and places the first runner. He might even run a rope through a runner. Catching sight of this practice earlier in the day, Majorie had called across 'What's all this yo-yoing then?' 'It's the Norwegian style', I said. 'You'll find out when you get there.' Fortunately she had to get on with throwing the dog sticks and Mike words of encouragement as he decided not to finish Jermyn Street but the top of Regent Street instead.

I could not even start Great Portland Street. I know it is not really a mantleshelf at all, as it says it is in the guidebook, but a long reach for a good edge. My fingertips did not even touch it after half-a-dozen attempts. So Norman took the lead, succeeded first time, put a runner in the crack and came down again, insisting that now I do it. On the second attempt, for some reason that cannot be physical, I reached the edge and pulled on to the ledge. Above here the crack itself leans up to a bulge above which it is just vertical. But the splendid bridging gives perfect balance until the little foot ledges disappear and it is all foot friction under the bulge with finger-tips jammed in a thinning crack.

To get past this little bulge it seemed necessary to lay back on the finger jam, but since I had put a nut in where most of the fingers ought to be, and trusting to the nut rather than the insecure digits, I snatched at the sling and pulled. This is cheating and nothing to be proud of. I know that Mike and Majorie's dog will never look me in the eye again. But the rest of the route was superb, its vertical line cut across by little edges and its

crack shaped inside, as if by the fit of a fist. Gill turned up just in time to get the pictures as though there'd never been a little improvization, but the dog had gone.

Late in the month this year Gill and I drove through the rain to Wales, hoping to be able to continue researching the routes first climbed by Tony Moulam, that redoubtable exponent of the verb 'to traverse'. Every sign in the heavy sky pointed us towards his Ordinary Route on Carreg Alltrem, a Diff on a steep, quick-drying crag. It was no longer raining as we drove up the forest road into the quiet valley of Cwm Penamnen and when we stepped out of the car opposite the crag, there was only the echoing sound of birdsong and the river. If everything in June is lush in its fullness, that can also include the river in a wet month. Wading the river to get to the crag must, I explained to Gill as she removed her boots, only add to the richness of the experience. Like finding that this route is not a Diff at all as it rises steeply leftwards with increasingly thin and technical moves on awkwardly placed handholds. Certainly the bulging traverse back right, hanging on to big wobbly blocks, would worry a Diff leader, although equally certainly the upper slab is delightfully Diff. Rumour has it that the present guidebook writer is considering the grade of Severe.

Back down at the car we absorbed the stillness and a bottle of Lambrusco. We shared a distinct feeling that the spirit of Pan was abroad in the valley, released by the alchemy of water, rock and wine. Then it was down to Tremadog for an evening taste of Moulam's Christmas Curry, the original top pitch of which is a wonderful variety of moves, now neglected by the *Selected Climbs'* preference for the Micah Finish.

The original finish gives an easy layback leading to a bold swing left round an arete as you hang off the spike at its top. An airy hand traverse and an awkward mantleshelf brings a comforting cluster of spikes within reach. But the wall above has polished little footholds leading to a delicate high step into the friction of a glacis, which gave each of us in turn cause to pause. The sun had gone off the crag and we were late for a simple feast waiting for us at Jim Perrin's house overlooking the line of crags we were on. Doris accepted our apologies with that quiet unflappable smile of hers and Jim agreed with Gill about the polish on Christmas

*Starting the original finish of Christmas Curry* (Gill Round).

*Starting the original finish of Christmas Curry* (Gill Round).

Curry as he poured out the wine. A gentle walk on the beach was needed in the morning.

These last two years the month has come to a climbing climax with my birthday party. Last year it was my fortieth birthday party. Anyone could come and everyone was invited. All they had to do was carry camping gear and wine up to Hollowstones below Scafell Crag. Climbing gear and food were optional. Six of us walked up from the Wasdale Head after three pints of Jennings on Friday night, leaving behind the Famous Persons gathering for the centenary celebrations for the climbing of Napes Needle. Even after setting off at 11.10 pm in shorts and vest, the sweat licked up by the steepness of Brown Tongue was hard to contend with.

In the morning the postman had come. My mum had sent me a banner that delicately reminded me of my age. John and Joëlle gave me an inflatable slice of birthday cake. The best birthday present was the clearness of the day and the dryness of the rock. Gill and I headed for an ascent of Scafell Pinnacle by Jones' Route Direct, while Kev and Barbie went with John and Joëlle into Lord's Rake for a ramble over the tops. Meanwhile the rest of the party was driving up to the treat of Brown Tongue in the heat of the day. Norman, nearing Hollowstones, said to Andy 'Is that Terry on CB?' 'No,' said John. 'The only CB he'd be on is a radio!'

John was right. Jones' Route Direct was just

**Left** *The author makes his first moves on the Ordinary Route, Carreg Alltrem* (Gill Round).

**Left** *The author reaches the top of Carreg Alltrem* (Gill Round).

the thing for Gill's first Lakes Severe. Positive holds on perfect rock quickly gets you into the centre of a serious expanse of cliff on a long rhythm of run-out after run-out. At the top of the Pinnacle we came out into the sunshine and sat a long time enjoying our isolation from the walkers passing by across the gap from our undercut summit.

Back at the camp we found that our tents seemed to have been pitched in the dark across a minor footpath that descends more directly from the crag. 'Look who's coming to your party, Terry!', Norman shouted across to us. Chris Bonington came running through saying 'Hello' to the upturned faces. 'It's David Craig!' Norman continued, as David and his son Neil came upon us with surprise. 'Did we arrange to meet here?' David asked, his memory recalling a birthday party invitation filed away in there somewhere. 'Yes, thanks

for coming. Bonington just passed through too'. David crossed himself in awkward reverence.

Let us allow the sunset to draw a veil over this particular evening's proceedings, so that we do not have to linger upon Kev eating his meal from the grass after a classic 'flip', or a certain Sheffield headteacher balancing on one leg with a pan of wine in an outstreched hand (he'd forgotten his mug again). The photographs are waiting their moment in the blackmail file. Next morning Norman led me, for some reason, up the *shortest* route on the crag, Botterill's Slab.

The climbing tunes you into its delicacy and its position on the edge of the cliff, whilst gradually increasing in difficulty as the holds get smaller and the thinking gets faster. Momentum is everything. In 1903 Fred Botterill, with big boots and rucksack, climbed

**Right** *Castle Helen after the sudden shower* (Terry Gifford).

**Above right** *At Castle Helen, Terry Gifford makes a careful descent* (Gill Round).

first with an ice-axe between his teeth, paused to raise his hat to a lady, found he had left his axe stuck in a crack below, downclimbed to hook it with a foot but instead knocked it out, traversed right but started on the wrong foot, so retreated and restarted before pulling through to have made the first ascent. Well, for me 83 years later with sticky boots and a rope above, momentum was everything.

Next we teamed up with David and Neil for an ascent of Slab and Groove, at least we teamed up with Neil, as he was about to begin seconding, persuading him to take a rope for us, since Norman was now feeling an injury sustained in some form of overbalancing. It is a bold and absorbing route, up and left across a draughts-board of slab and round its breezy edge to a steep wall that hangs above the slab. Its fine exposure and the continuously bantering company made a fitting end to our alternative celebrations above Wasdale that weekend.

This year the party was to have been below Cloggy, but after weeks of rain we reverted to Cwm Glas. Gill and I met up with Tim, John and David to spend a wet night in the Pass before searching for dry rock on Anglesey's Castle Helen on the Saturday, whilst the others were driving up to meet us. Tim once again organized with relish the two abseils to sea level and David then traversed away left to find Lighthouse Arete. It is a route with one spectacular crux — an entry into a groove that hangs, undercut, over the sea. David walked his feet up under its lip to enable him to reach into the groove for huge white chunks of quartz and a pull into its vertical body-bite. As David belayed he was watching seals lifting and falling under the water. When I climbed up to him I was mumbling about my having snatched at holds the size of elephant's molars.

After a drenching from a sudden shower on Blanco and an epic traverse left into Lighthouse Arete, we returned to the rain of the Pass. A search of the car parks failed to reveal Norman's car, so we decided that he, Kev and Barbie had not come. Whilst we sat wondering where they were, drinking the Isle of Jura malt whisky Dave gave me for my birthday, they sat high up in Cwm Glas drinking Kev's 'chum juice' and wondering where we were. So, unaware of the curses being spoken over my head on the hill above, I missed my own birthday party. Anyway, Norman said later, they enjoyed it better without me.

> For in June there's a red rose bud
> And that's the flower for me
> But often I have snatched at that red rose bud
> And gained the willow tree
> And gained the willow tree.

**Above** *Gill Round crosses the river to Carreg Alltrem* (Terry Gifford).

**Right** *The author belaying Norman Elliott on Great Portland Street* (Gill Round).

*Dream of White Horses is in spectacular surroundings* (Gill Round).

Terry Gifford was born in June 1946 with one foot in the Fens and the other on top of Castle Hill, Cambridge. A move to Sheffield as a student resulted in long-term residency and short days on short crags. A recognized exponent of 'Soft Rock' writing, Terry Gifford has contributed regularly to the outdoor magazines. He teaches English at Bretton Hall College of Higher Education and recently had a collection of climbing and outdoor poems, *The Stone Spiral*, published by Giant Steps.

# Twelve Julys

## DAVID CRAIG

June ceases to flame and shine with its precise sting like a burning-glass. The huge dry wind that rushed up Wasdale and blew grit into our eyes as we dropped down Broad Stand after balancing up Birkett's immaculate slab, then moved round to the loom of the East Buttress to weave our ways up Phoenix, has died back into the doldrum of July. The exact apex of the watershed between the months occurs at the top of Bill Peascod's Long Tom on Grey Crag, Birkness Combe.

On a rasping April day I had sat by the fire in the Fell and Rock hut on the eastern slope of Buttermere and scanned the route book line by line. Work on the Buttermere guide was just getting under way and who knew what neglected crannies might come to light in the ballpen jottings — some facetious, some jubilant, some plain factual — by the generations of members? On page 15 I read that on 19 March 1953 A. J. J. Moulam and J. M. Barr had added a new second pitch to Long Tom: 'Take the steep crack up the L wall, awkward exit. Then step L onto face again to finish on easy ridge.' When I mention this to Bill, he agrees that the route 'needed straightening out' — a rare concession for one fiercely proud, and rightly so, of his lines.

As June expires and July begins to brood, I hike up into the Combe with Cameron Self, an excellent young poet from Norwich, who had tried to break upwards out of the flatlands as a student at Hull by joining the climbing club, but had rarely, he says, done more than 'stand about in Langdale, looking up at Raven Crag in the rain'. Now he is gazing all around him at the massive shoulders of the Buttermere Fells, the lake shrinking to a large-scale map below us, the vistas up Honister and down Crummock Water. The scene is a little greyed and blurred by a moistening air-stream which the corrie seems to be sucking in and exhaling in great breaths. Before we move round to reconnoitre the 'new' finish to Long Tom, an imposing VS detains us — not a common thing on Grey, which Wilfred Noyce truly described

as 'sunsplashed and restful' with 'fine possibilities of gymshoe wandering'. That was in 1940. Soon Dexter Wall and Fortiter had announced a bolder approach to Grey. Just after the War two climbers mentioned in no other List of First Ascents found this handsome pitch at the very corner of Mitre Buttress. To the left of the comfortable, slabby tracts explored by A. C. Pigou and his Cambridge

*Cameron Self abseiling* (Author's collection).

young men during the Great War, a dark wall leans over the scree chute. You step left on to it and at once your centre of gravity trembles uncomfortably; balancing demands a concentration of the will. A staircase of ledges rears abruptly towards the skyline. The edges are good and positive but each riser is steep enough to ease you remorselessly outwards until you mantel on to the next tread. At the top I take off my new JB helmet, bought to replace the trusty item which the past decade has crunched and cracked beyond usefulness, and perch it on the stance beside me to let my head cool off. As I bring up Cameron, a gust buffets through the gully, snatches up my helmet and lobs it down the 100 ft drop into the scree, which it hits with a clunk like the tortoise hitting Aeschylus on the skull (it killed

him). When I retrieve it, the shattered white blaze on the scarlet paint is as big as a boiled egg and I rarely wear it again.

By the time we reach Long Tom, via Harrow Wall and the lovely stretching delicacies of Suaviter, not only the crag but also everything else is grey — the scree fans, the lowering clouds, the metallic surfaces of the twin lakes, which dim and vanish and reappear through hill fog like dry steam. Four hundred feet of climbing has set off that lovely flow when you feel you could climb through sunset and midnight to next day's dawning. I climb Long Tom's lower parts a little faster than the fog, which is now filling tidally. Subtle holds entice the fingers upwards; it would all be rated excellent if a mucky gully did not lour in from the right, leaking and oozing. It is Tom's fault:

*Spectacular scenery at Gimmer Crack* (Jerry Rawson).

he turns out to be a surly stone gnome who pees his bed continually — uncomfortable for him but he does not mind as long as he spites us. He stands at the back of a square stance close-carpeted with turf. Above his head is a dirty vault, its stones jammed unconvincingly together. Cameron comes up and we speculate about how much help the gnome will be if we stand on his head (as Bill recommends in the guidebook) and 'ascend the bulge above, treating some doubtful blocks with care.' It looks like a bad joke — a malign gnomic wheeze, much harder than 'Severe (hard)' and much more rickety than it must have been when Bill and G. G. MacPhee (pioneer of Gimmer Crack and Deer Bield Crack) explored it 30 years ago. I hug the gnome, paw at the blackened flanges, back down and wipe my hands on my trousers. Just below us the image of the combe has wiped as blank as a switched-off television. Greyish tendrils blow upwards past us. Cameron's long face (he is a professional pessimist) has taken on the look of one who does not expect to see Norfolk again in this life. We seem to be standing like the last two people in the world, marooned on the top of a skyscraper as the waters rise.

I edge along the wall above the stance and feel round the arete. Is this what Moulam meant? My fingers curl round a knobby jug. Here is the acme of commitment — a move into the unseen and unknown. But Moulam and Barr left their frail clue and Moulam's rock-sense was, on his record, as fine as anyone's. I step up, grip, swing round. It is technically comfortable, only the swimming white blindness of everything makes it awesome. It is not hard to perch in balance and spy out the next moves upwards, and they are imposing. A clean-cut crack splits the wall, homing on a niche, cleaving on into the cloudy upper reaches. I jam with both my hands and they lodge like dovetails. Pull up, smear with the feet, pull up, jam a toe. It feels more like gritstone climbing, but the hands suffer less. A faintly precarious half-mantel gets me into the niche; step up and jam and lay-away with growing ease until the crag lies back into a rickle of boulders. Tied on, I look out into an ocean of wool. Cameron's voice reaches me like the last faint calls of a castaway as his ship recedes. When he calls up, 'What do you do?' and I shout back, 'Jam it — it's really solid — easier than it looks', his reply floats up, 'I've never jammed!' For some minutes I play him

like a fish, gauging his progress or resistance by the tension of the rope. But it is no good: he is perceiving the wall as impassable. After a shouted conference I set up an abseil and swing down the gully, pendule out on to the face to retrieve my gear, and in half an hour we are crunching downwards to Gatesgarth under the sombre overcast.

From now on it is no good expecting the radiance of high summer. The sycamore and hawthorn leaves are darkening from the luminous lettuce-green of their youth last month; the verges of the tracks, and the canal towpath near home, are filling up with the surly leafage of nettles; thickets of rose-bay willow herb have replaced the white lacework of cow-parsley and may-blossom; the fell-sides have grown a scaly hide of braken. Advancing middle-age and natural melancholia alert me slightly prematurely to the signs that the British summer is levelling out, beginning to fray and sag, too heartbreakingly soon after its prime. But Bill and I defy all this on a clammy 6 July at Shepherd's when the sky is more white than blue, the sweat won't evaporate, and we climb all day coated in it as though buttered ready for grilling. 510 ft of rock, scarcely a move below 4B, our combined ages 114: by the end we are wearied by the continual coiling and uncoiling and downward clattering on slatey paths but utterly attuned and content.

We start up North Crag Buttress, which has intrigued Bill for 30 years, since he put up Eve. His climbing diary for 11 August 1951 claims proudly for that route: 'This is the first ascent of North Buttress', boldy underlined in ink. He never attempted the awkward, chunky, frontal line of the Buttress itself, which took the best efforts of the next wave, three years later. It has been daunting me for years, the fault of the old guide from the far-off days when you were allowed to describe climbs and use words like 'green' and 'dubious-looking' to evoke the rock itself. The Buttress has not quite become one of my pet challenges, grimacing at me in the small hours of the morning (like Sword of Damocles and Perhaps Not and Deer Bield Buttress and Cenotaph Corner and The Link on Lochnagar and...). But I have always known it is there, demanding to be tackled, as I slink past to easier things. As I work my way up the long first pitch, it is like learning to climb again — how steep a facet will support the feet by friction alone, how cramped a hold (three fingers' breadth? Two?) will be enough to pull

**Below** *The author on Pitch 2, Adam, Shepherd's Crag* (John Wilkinson).

up on? Little blackened saw-edges have to be trusted, the occasional small hex lodged none too securely. I'm never at ease, never enjoying myself, until the crucial traverse back right faces me with a long stride supported by nothing better than a finger or two stuck into a hole with broken lips. Now I have played myself in, the previous 80 ft have charged me up and reminded me vividly what good traction can be got on little features. Confidence wells as palpably as the tide filling up an inlet, and I step and pull, step and pull with the good feeling of singing in tune until I am perched on the eyrie of the stance and I can look out with cleansed, rejuvenated vision across the reaches of Derwentwater, oyster-grey and silky under an opaque sky.

Bill has called up more often than usual 'What's it like?', and I've been answering, less sunnily than usual, 'Not easy... quite awkward... sharp but thin,' and other breathless ambiguities. On vertical moves he is liable to call up 'Take my weight!', and I never do, and he never needs it, but today the familiar shout makes me fear more keenly than usual that *this* might be a route when his heart, damaged by a massive coronary ten years before, suddenly gives way and leaves him dangling from my Sticht-plate. But all goes happily and he joins me on the stance in high good-humour at following the redoubtable line at last. The first 100 ft of it, anyway. Now 'Step left and ascend the overhanging groove.' How quickly said, barely a line of print. I have been craning doubtingly up at it, I know it will put a brake on me, and it does. You stand under the mouth of a passage like a leaded valley in a slate roof. It is defended by an eave. Move the feet up, sway back, eel over, reach up, pull up (all this in fantasy, you understand) — on what? The valley sides are smooth as the hull of a foundering ship must look to those cast overboard. In the joint up there a thick old hand-forged peg, or so it looks, offers its eye, big enough for a finger, asking for a krab and a sling, round which the desperate hand could clench... I must not do that — I will not do that — I *will* free-climb this classic. I just can't. I glare at it for quarter of a useless hour, fidgeting upwards, groping at the sides of the valley, getting nowhere, explaining away the impasse to Bill, who can see it all anyway. Finally I swallow my pride — a bitter gulp — and quest off rightwards to escape. Still the climb is not over and I sketch incredibly steep

moves up what I later find to be PS (E1 5b) until at last I give the buttress my best and monkey across a slab to the sanctuary of an oak.

As we eat mint cake and butties, the book tells us that the Slab Finish was the original line, done by Peter Greenwood and E. Mallinson. To finish directly, Peter had to come back a few weeks later with his 'bodyguard' Pete Whitwell (as Mike Thompson calls him in Paul Ross's 1965 guide) and Don Whillans. Even that spearhead team needed two pegs for aid to surmount the overhang and the groove above, so who am I to scourge myself for failing? We are in top gear now, if not overdrive, and I point Bill at Paul Ross's companion to Eve, Adam, whose handsome swarthy front I first climbed on an early visit to Shepherd's with my eldest son, Pete. The black faces marbled with Stilton green have the beauty of barbarous jewellery, jet and turquoise combined in jagged patterns. Chunks have acute edges, like hardwood logs that have surrendered more to the hammering of the axe than its splitting. Thick canines stick up, black yet undecayed, good for decades yet. Puckered surfaces, wizened like leather turned to stone, offer wrinkles perfect for edging. Trees here are bonsai — 7 ft hollies, 12 ft oaks, with the squat trunks and muscled limbs of dwarfs. The holly in the middle of Adam is unforgettable, stability incarnate amongst all these verticals. Its satin-grey bole welcomes fingers, arms, slings, a harbour where it would be delightful to spend a day, contented as a full-fed buzzard, though the guidebooks invite you to steam past it on a 90 ft run-out and Roper, Eilbeck and Cram point you straight up the wall above it, as though directness was a virtue. Paul Ross had noticed this and objected to it: 'It goes out right, doesn't it?' he asked me, annoyed, and so it does, moving towards an arete which drops its great blade darkly against the gleam of the southern sky. The magnetism of that profile draws you irresistibly into an area which seems improbably steep, as does the wall above it, but both these passages offer finger-jugs so angled and so spaced that you swing up them in ecstasy untainted by desperation, each surge so free and dynamic you wish it would never end. Bill, proud father of Eve, wonders jealously if the upstart Adam was any harder at the finish and it has to be said that the slanting cleft on Eve pitch 3 makes a handrail more secure than Adam's mini-flakes. But the contrast, such as it is, is minor beside the fact that both routes soar to their very finishes on the solid turf belvedere where the Borrowdale woodlands end in mid-air and a gulf of pure space hollows northwards towards Bassenthwaite.

By now we had embarked on a tour of the VS classics that had been found while Bill was overseas. Among the tall trees at the north end, where midges are gathering as though the lake was a loch, we climb Vesper — traversing at its best, more or less unprotectable after the bulge, so that both leader and second can savour the naked daring of the pioneers Greenwood and Ross as they spy out ledges no broader than the spine of a guidebook or hook fingerends into ragged sockets to sustain strides at the full reach of the legs. I climb quickly, either because Bill is holding the rope one-handed while he swats midges or because I do not have the strength to hang about on so steep a wall. He climbs with the nimbleness of the man who was first along the traverses on Cleopatra (Buckstone How), Delilah (High Crag), and Jezebel (Newlands). Surely we are finished for the day? The fells are featureless in the haze and the last walkers have gone from the water-meadows between Grange and the lake. But we have to contour back the length of the crag to reach the car and as we pause in the stony bay at the left of the Chamonix area, the narrow mouth of Kranzic Crack says 'Climb me'. I have been wondering for years how good the jams are, so up we go, revelling in the narrowness of the flake top, finding the moves off it on to and along the wall to be at the most taxing and finely-whetted end of VS/4c. It takes the exact placing of a toe or finger to unlock each problem and we are reminded of last month's climb along the more delicate edgings on pitches 6, 9, and 13 of the Pillar Girdle, the longest climb in England. Back at the foot we unbuckle harnesses and unlace PA's in a happy trance, looking at each other and laughing in wonderment at the desire for rock that has prolonged the day so far into the phase of hunger and fatigue (and so long past opening time).

From now on the month is steeped in moisture — drunk, perspired, exuded by the crags and teemed down out of the clouds. On the 7th the sky lours, blurring the summits of High Pike and Red Stile. The mosses in Birkness Combe are gemmed with droplets, the stains of seepage are as dark as Guinness.

On a reconnaissance for the guidebook, Rick Graham shepherds me firmly across the boundary between my half of the territory (up to HVS) and his. On Eagle Crag this occupies the rock around the impending cracks of Carnival and Hugh Banner's Direct Finish to Bill Peascod's Fifth Avenue. The start of the Avenue should be mine but the difficult move on to the wall of pitch 2 (old pitch 4) flummoxes me. I cannot believe a wet PA would stay put on so rounded a knob, Rick takes over, and from then on I have to wait patiently, staring at the mortifying feature, while he rains down clots of sodden earth as he digs out slots for wires. (It is the only Peascod move I have ever failed to make.) At least I can *see* him and enjoy the work of a master-climber at close quarters when we move on up to have a look at the Direct Finish. This cleft through a beetling overhang looks impossibly steep and it is a sight to see Rick hanging by one hand, probing holes for runners, leaning back onto the air as though it is a deck-chair, minute after minute. When I try to follow, my arms feel as weak as a child's and I simply ask him to winch me up. It is a comfort when he upgrades it to E1/5b, which is more or less my limit — although the 5b crack on Carnival incites me to a burst of unaided climbing and I lay-away from its knife-edge so vigorously that the pads of my fingers ache afterwards as we zig leftwards towards the great gut of Central Chimney, then zag back across a wall barely equipped with fingerholds.

As we coil and review the routes, we hear the dreadful flutter of wind ruffling fast round a falling body. It sounds like a climber's clothes flapping as he falls. I look round: nothing. It comes again and two peregrines, close together, are in semi-free fall, a few feet out from the stance, letting gravity rule for a second, wrenching out of it with incredible athletic tensioning of the wings to cut widely off and up and over the summit ridge, streaks of brown and white fire flaming against the damp shade of the north face and the colourless sky.

The summer is set in its ways now, no longer a revelation, as I find when I next walk up for a work-out on 'my' crag — my 'secret' crag — a mile from home. It is a ragged limestone edge, no classic battlement like Twistleton or Giggleswick or Malham Right Wing, more an assortment of low, ruined towers like chunks of abandoned concrete, but seamed with fierce problems and wholly to my taste as a practice ground because it was not built, it evolved, rowans and ashes spring from its deeper clefts, and as you rest on top looking northwest to Coniston Old Man and Bow Fell across a tussocky plateau, you may see a roedeer, head up, ears pricked, in silhouette against the mountains. One limestone forehead bulges into a split overhang and this is my 5b problem. Pull up on shallow mouths (one of them liable to drool), bridge widely and go for the split with the right hand. It closes on your flesh like pliers, it hurts and it will not work unless it does — resist the temptation to hang off for a rest, pull on up, go for the boss on the left with your other hand, extract your right and entrust yourself to the air in one sheer swing, rock over on to the skull and mantel up... All right, 5a perhaps, but I never manage it at the first shot, or the second.

This evening the problems feel like work or sleep-walking, because the verve seems to have drained out of nature. Summer's first flush has dulled. When I get home, Anne is amazed by my hangdog face and thinks I have had bad news or seen an accident. Next day I write out as a poem this vision of the season's change:

### Doldrum

In less than a month our fastness,
The hidden vale on the fell's flank,
Has wasted under Saturn.
Dust from the planet of age
Has dowsed the sycamore's flourish,
Withered the whin-flowers,
Emptied the larks from the air,
Choked the throat of the curlew.
It has petrified the bracken.

The bracken bides its time,
Scaly and uniform, tough green pelt
Of a single pack, the rat-plant
Consuming the upland. Beyond,
The mountains in June were oven-stones
Swollen with secret fires.
Now they are pale-blue dreams,
Barely-remembered pasts. A ban
Has fallen upon the hill.

The leveret and the roe
Absorb to brown shadows.
The carrion crow is a branch
On a ring-barked tree.
The pipit's nest is a wisp
Of last year's wind-gleanings.

Now my brain's screen blanks,
Every silvery image dulled,
As the fell dwindles to an islet
Becalmed in faceless haze,
Helplessly waiting for the ebb
At the year's slack water.

On the 9th I go to Swindale with Rob Crawshaw to do one or two of its harder and more recent routes, post Charlie Wilson and post Harold Drasdo. The Nymph is as good as we hoped — a rising traverse leading to a bulging crack which demands quick combinings of lay-away and mantel — but Garm is a revelation. For some reason Rob believes me to be a connoisseur of obscure grot and he is not surprised that I am intent on finding an 'excavated slab'. 'Excavated' makes us look for a dug-out start or base. It turns out to be a sweep of rock as pale (after its stripping in 1966) as the newly-shaven cheeks of a once-bearded face. I pad up it from ledge to tree root to half-way terrace and shout down warm words to which Rob responds in a tone both cynical and humouring. In this semi-artificial environment I feel like a bear on a Mappin terrace and he is my tolerant keeper. But he warms to the route, leads the taxing wall above the terrace in his 'super-cool' and unerring style, and does seem to concede afterwards that there are excellences to be found in byways of the Lakes.

From the 11th to the 14th I am in Sheffield, my annual venture around the fringes of that hot-bed with its latest news of Paul Nunn's sayings and Ron Fawcett's or Jerry Moffatt's doings, Birtles's disenchanted move over to the new mania, parascending, the intrigues to shift the BMC franchise from *Climber* to *High*. Although an ocean of moorland lies just over the rim of Stanage, Sheffield climbing, to someone from Wordsworth country, feels wholly urban. When I stop off *en route* to work out at Millstone Edge, I see a perfect subject for a Hogarth of the climbing scene. Beneath the blunt prow of Master's Edge which Fawcett has recently whitened with his great chalked paws, this fashion-plate is standing with turquoise singlet, wasp-striped Italian nylon tights, red-laced Firés and gaping chalk-bag. He inspects his soles, has a dip and looks round to see who is watching. He sets hands to rock, moves up three feet, paralysis sets in, he grunts, drops off, shakes out, looks round, clambers a little more... As I move on to the Scoop (described by Nunn with amiable pedantry as 'D 2b'), he is still deep in his narcissistic rite, and probably still is.

Sheer towers of grit and castles of limestone are waiting a little further on, and so are grizzled friends who first climbed here before hexes were invented and still have a handful of fine items on their agendas (and always will). 'Let's start at Willersley,' they say, 'then drive round to High Tor if we're going well.' Left to myself I might never have tried Willersley. 'The crag is approached via iron gates near the Cromford junction' sounds grimly urban. 'Access is strictly forbidden, for obscure religious and other reasons' might have incited me, as Nunn doubtless meant it to. The crag is excellent, towering parallel with mature trees. The Great Corner offers the reasonably-angled start that I need to adjust my early morning

*The author on* Wharncliffe Prow *(Author's collection).*

nerves and then I please myself, leading the first pitch of Porthole Wall. It is steep enough to press its broad stone hand against your chest, forcing you to move with the chary deliberateness of a bomb-disposal squad. After 70 ft of that I am happy to follow Norman Elliott past the pothole to a dizzy perch and a finish amongst jungle threaded with sinuous paths, an unkempt Avon Gorge without the prams or ice-cream vans. In the shade the earth is still darkened by dew. Two hours later, High Tor glares like a threshing floor tilted to the vertical above the chimney pots of Matlock. The temperature must have peaked near 80° and the honeyed air seems to run down our skins. When I lead the jamming pitch of Skylight, my hands slither as though I have been handling fresh fish — two steps upwards, one downwards. The sun roasts the back of my neck, a Mediterranean dazzle all around, the horrendous battlement of Castellan jutting on my right. Here is a great beauty of climbing, that ordinary climbers can enjoy themselves on the very verge of an area, can see close up the minutest features of a route, that represents the summit of the sport.

The shade of the upper chimney on Skylight is actually welcome: strange after years of huddling into shelter from chilling winds. It makes High Tor feel like Buis les Baronnies. Up above, Terry, Norman and I walk about dazed, in a lush beauty-spot equipped with a café. With local knowledge they have carried up small change to buy mugs of tea but now, at the very end of a sweltering Saturday, we feast for almost nothing. They offer us, free, slice after slice of bedraggled strawberry cake whose fruit and cream will not last another day and we gobble it up and wash it down with scalding draughts until the plate is empty. It makes me feel I have stepped through the looking-glass: there is nothing like this to assuage you as you haul out on to the top of Gimmer!

I am in Sheffield partly to climb as many pinnacles as possible with Terry, photographed by Ian Smith, for a section of a book (*Native Stones*). An impure experience, you may say, but good climbing shots are almost impossible to get on the spur of the moment; they have to be set up. So we burrow into the steamy woods at Wharncliffe and monkey about happily on the rocks that look blackened by industrial smoke, too little visited to be rubbed through again to their native red. We spiral up

*The mood of the edges and hills is captured in this atmospheric shot of Bamford Edge in the Peak District* (John Woodhouse).

the Prow and leap across to the mainland from its top, then move along to sample the blocky natural masonry where J. W. Puttrell launched gritstone climbing a century ago and gave his lines stately names like Puttrell's Progress. But the hard core of our project centres on Rivelin Needle. It was once called Rivelin Steeple and this change pleases me because I believe that these quarried pinnacles (at Tegness, Wharncliffe, Mow Cop, Wilton) are totems, therefore the phallic sense of 'needle' is more apt than the churchy 'steeple'. This tower rising out of the bracken jungle is blunt and bald, with few weaknesses. The nearer we get, the more it repulses me.

We go for Croton Oil, though 'go for' is too dynamic for my nervy gropes and fumbles. Terry is all patience as I move up to the last substantial feature, a rounded 2 in ledge, where I stand for what seems days like the Frog Footman, immobile with my feet turned outwards. I eye the next cluster of chalk marks, a poor straight–up edge, a slightly better one above it, both apparently the keys

to the passage up and left to a coign of vantage profiled against the pale blue hazy sky. I inch upwards, stretch fingers for edge 1, sketch a sideways pull, my sweaty extremities slipping. This farce is repeated three times until my will turns soft as a rotten apple and I back down wishing that I was Whillans, that I had started climbing at fifteen — anything other than I really am.

> Self-yeast of spirit a dull dough sours. I see
> The lost are like this and their scourge to be
> As I am mine, their sweating selves; but worse.

But as Hopkins also says,

> Soul, self, come, poor Jackself, I do advise
> You, jaded, let be; call off thoughts awhile
> Elsewhere; leave comfort root-room...

Next morning we are back. Ian has arrived, slung about with cameras. Now it *must* be done. But this is not all that is going for me: yesterday's failure turned the Needle from a

bogey into a material challenge. Now at least it will not be aura that beats me but only (only!) the stature of the rock. Terry stands on the plinth. I move up briskly to the ledge, carrying his chalk-bag. Was this huge ethical concession the key? I leave the last sure footing and friction up to edge 1, try the leverage, feel how slight it is, and retreat — tactically — wailing to Terry, 'It's no use — this place is for good climbers.' The faithful lad shouts up, 'You *are* a good climber.' What Ibsen calls 'the saving lie'. Next time I feel together, unified; I can think what to do and do what I think of. Toes stick on the merest worn layer-ends in the sandstone, edge 1 eases me readily upwards to edge 2, my floury fingers grapple firmly on to it and I am toeing leftwards towards that perch, all tremor gone, my muscles flexing smoothly. The knowledge that

**Left** *The author looks for a secure foothold on Wharncliffe Prow* (Author's collection).

**Below** *The author leaps from Wharncliffe Prow* (Gill Round).

**Right** *The author and Terry Gifford on Croton Oil, Rivelin Needle* (Ian Smith).

**Far right** *Bill Peascod on Pitch 1, Green Fingers, Nagg's Slab (Car-park Crag), Borrowdale* (Author's collection).

I am at my optimum has me whooping wordlessly, hardly pausing on the bracket, jamming on upwards between the rickety final flakes with a fierce pleasure, almost, as they sandpaper the backs of my tingling hands.

It had taken my utmost in nerve, balance, finger strength, technique, and really I do not want to separate these 'faculties'. The nerve to balance up, trusting the feet, then lay-away leftwards with right arm tensed to hold weight on the assumption that as the fingers took full load the traction would get good before the toes slid backwards off — this was all one conception and one movement — conceived of too much since yesterday, but at least it won through to actual experience today.

On the way home across the Snake Pass the car rides on an air-cushion of happy retrospect while the sky bruises over and practises a few warning drops. July has some sweets left of a dampish kind. In the newly defoliated Car-park Crags in Borrowdale with Bill Peascod, we climb Green Fingers on Nagg's Slab and dig out a new route, Stingray, on Beth's Crag (16 and 18 July); then an epic voyage up Y Gully on Haystacks, Buttermere, where moisture never ceases to irrigate the lady's mantle and saxifrage even in the middle of an anti-cyclone (22 July). On the 17th we had outsmarted the water by arranging to climb Cleopatra for the photographer at noon, no earlier, so that her tawny front ('with Phoebus' amorous kisses black, And wrinkled deep in time') was already being sunned, drying out the seep and sharpening the image. And that *was* a highlight, Bill girding himself up to lead the pocketed traverse 31 years after he was the first to cross it.

A few miles down the dale from Buckstone How, the month glided coolly to its end as Anne and I rowed over Crummock Water, glad to have found a perfect bed-and-breakfast place

at Rannerdale. We had to suss Ling Crag for the guidebook. It is a landmark — one lone

hummock of Skiddaw slate whose forepaw stretches out into water pure as liquid rock. We climb the Slabs, where the glacier has graved an old volcanic rib to a gradual angle, corrugated now and again by rounded sills where you must reach up, find nothing, and pad upwards with faith in friction. This is awkward because I have brought two left-footed EBs for Anne and have to lend her one of my Firés, so she climbs in odd PA's and I in one Firé and one Walsh fell-trainer. Then she gives me a top-rope down the precipitous northern side where some force has torn out rock in jagged masses, creating VS and harder pitches. The wind is planing across the water now with almost an autumnal edge, tinged with the firmness of apples and the rustiness of tarnishing bracken.

Twelve July's have been packed into the above pages, as though this month has been stretched to an entire year, and in all these twelve years, according to my records, I have spent only one memorable day on rock between 22 July and 31 July. It is a shame and a crime that English holidays are distorted so that the House of Lords (and a few hangers-on in the Commons) can shoot grouse from 12 August, partridges from 1 September, and pheasants from 1 October. By mid-July rainfall is markedly increasing, the nights are cooler, gales arrive, rending tents and setting fishing boats adrift — and at last the children are given their holidays. Late May to late July is our prime season and it is then that the schools and colleges should be on vacation so that the families can go into the mountains when the sun is at its height and the days are longest.

David Craig comes from Aberdeen. He began climbing on Lochnagar and Beinn a Bhuird in 1952, but did not take it up seriously until 1974, when his children began to go climbing in Langdale and Borrowdale with their school. Since then he has climbed mainly in the Lakes, Cornwall, Wester Ross, and the Peak, with two visits to the Italian Dolomites. He lives in Cumbria and teaches Creative Writing at the University of Lancaster. He wrote *Native Stones* (Secker) and has co-authored the Buttermere section of the Fell & Rock Buttermere/Eastern Fells guidebook.

# *August: Spirit of Alpinism*

## ROB COLLISTER

August is not the best of months to climb in British hills. It could aptly be called The Month of the Midge. Let the wind drop, or the sun sink behind a shoulder of the mountain, and up and down the Western seaboard of Britain a cloud of midges will appear on cue. Insect repellant is no answer, for it merely drives the creatures down your shirt, up your trouser legs or, worst of all, into your hair. Midges are a potential problem all summer, but in August they seem to reach an annual peak of ferocity and resilience. It is an obvious time to migrate, and if there are midges in the Alps, I have yet to be troubled by them.

By convention, the alpine year is neatly segmented. July and August are for climbing; April and May are for ski-touring; winter lasts from 21 December to 21 March. In between is limbo. Of course, that is nonsense. You can climb in the Alps at *any* time of year, and if you like a bit of adventure, you may actually prefer to do so out of season. Be that as it may, when I started climbing everyone went to the Alps in August, so *I* went to the Alps in August; and since everyone seemed to go to Chamonix, I, too, went to Chamonix. In fact, we were four, and because we all climbed VS at Stanage and in Wales, we had a high opinion of ourselves. For our debut we chose the Forbes Arete on the Chardonnet, which we thought rather beneath us for its technical difficulties are negligible, but it would be useful training and acclimatization. In the event we discovered that, despite a few days in Scotland the previous March, we were not very competent on snow or ice, some of us were not at all fit, and though we knew we should move together most of the time on the rock, in practice it did not feel as safe as we would have liked. In short, we were a fairly typical party of British novices and as a result, like many before us, we were benighted. There was a violent thunderstorm during the night and it snowed heavily. Mick Guilliard had a polythene bag; the rest of us put on our cagoules, stuck our feet in our rucksacks and

sat it out. We were frightened and miserable. Next day, after a harrowing (and unnecessary) jump from the lip of a bergschrund; we descended to the valley somewhat chastened.

Our next climb, a short rock route on the Moine, was relatively uneventful. Emboldened by this success we decided to try the east face of the Grépon, a much longer rock climb pioneered by Geoffrey Winthrop Young and Joseph Knubel before the First World War. At

*With the Alpine Ice Club, tackling the north face of Aiguille de Triocet* (Rob Ferguson).

*Impressive skyline on the Chardonnet-Forbes arete* (Rob Collister).

first all went well; though we did find
ourselves climbing grade IV rock in the dark to
reach the hut. This was the Rochers Rouges
bivouac, an amazing construction attached to
the mountain by a web of wire cables, with a
view through the floorboards into space. The
climbing next day was interesting and technical
on firm, rough granite. We managed to find
the way with only occasional errors and
climbing as two ropes of two ensured that we
did not move too slowly. It was beginning to
feel as though the summit could not be far
away when, out of the blue, disaster struck.
Not a natural disaster, like being hit by a stone
or struck by lightning but a human one, almost
as dire in its consequences. When things are
going badly on a climb, often the second is
noticeably more optimistic than the leader:
'Looks like a good hold a few feet above you',
or 'If you can get across to the right, it looks a
doddle', and so on. But the converse can also
be true, especially on a long climb. While the
leader is enjoying the intricacies of route-
finding, impelled upwards and onwards by his
own momentum, the second has time to look
around, to brood and worry. That was what

happened on the Grépon. I had reached the
top of a pitch, belayed and called 'Up you
come'. There was a pause. Then someone
shouted, 'Come back down. We've got to
retreat'. 'What?' I was incredulous.
'Why?' 'The weather's breaking.' I looked up
the glacier to a few cumulus clouds on the
horizon behind the Grandes Jorasses. Even now
I do not know quite what induced this panic in
the rear. Maybe it was the thought of the
Knubel Crack not far above, on which the axe-
cling technique, recently re-invented in
Scotland as 'hooking' and 'torquing', was
extensively employed on the first ascent.
Maybe the notorious seracs which threaten a
descent of the Nantillons glacier had grown
preposterously dangerous in the imagination of
ignorance. Whatever the reason, I was one and
they were three, and they were not coming
up. Fuming, but with my head of steam
already evaporating, I abseiled down and tried
to argue the point. No good. The others were
sheepish, but adamant. Down it had to be.

Now abseiling is a lengthy business at the
best of times. If you are a party of four, and
not very slick at finding anchors, and the knot

more than once jams when you pull the ropes down, it is very time-consuming indeed. Before we knew it we were settling down for our second unplanned bivouac in three routes. This time we had a stove and pot so at least we could spend the night brewing up. Alas, someone dropped the pot, so it was cold water after all, and nothing to do but curl up into a foetal position and wait for morning. I had a down jacket, but that did not do much for legs and feet, and the rope only kept out some of the cold seeping up from the rock beneath. Being a clear night it felt, and probably was, colder than our night in the storm, and I made a mental note to buy myself a poly bag. In the morning after a frugal breakfast, we continued on our way. By now we had lost the route of ascent, but we could see the Envers hut below us and were making for that. We had been scrambling down easy rock for a while when we came to a steep snow gully and set up another abseil from a small rock spike. Mick and John abseiled down, and I followed. Whether the loop slipped off the spike, or the spike itself snapped, I do not know. But one moment I was abseiling down a fixed rope, the next I was attached to nothing, shooting head first, on my back, down the gully. Sideways over a protruding rock I slid, right way up through some soft snow, head first again down a sheet of ice, wondering when something decisive would happen and vaguely registering the faces of Mick and John Hamilton, mouths agape. Suddenly, unexpectedly, I was myself again, stationary, just short of an overhanging rock wall that dropped into a gaping bergschrund. Picking myself up; I brushed some of the snow off my clothes and remarked, 'That's one way of getting down, I suppose.' Then I felt sick and faint and had to lean against the gully wall.

I had fallen 120 ft with nothing to show for it but a knee which was painful but had not yet begun to stiffen. More serious seemed to be the loss of my ice-axe, which had vanished. The next abseil, when Pete Hughes had climbed down to join us, was, I suppose, therapeutic in the same way as remounting a horse after falling off. But I did not enjoy it one bit. The anchor was a single peg (and we were not very experienced at placing pegs) and the abseil itself was free for the length of the rope, with a pendulum swing at the bottom to reach the lower lip of the bergschrund. Our progress thence down the glacier was slow.

*The east face of the Grépon* (Rob Collister).

The lack of an axe made the snow slopes dangerous and to bend my knee was increasingly painful. Soon I could not bend it at all and was forced to accept that I simply could not walk the whole way down. My first Alpine season ended ignominiously, but not unenjoyably, with a helicopter ride from the Envers hut down to Chamonix.

For reasons I do not understand, instead of putting me off Alpine climbing for good, this inauspicious start made me determined to do better next time. When next I went to the Alps I had three more Scottish winters and two small expeditions to the Hindu Kush behind me. I had learned many lessons in Apinism the hard way, but having survived them, chiefly by good fortune, I felt far more assured in the mountains. The techniques of travelling on glaciers, moving together on mixed terrain and cutting steps on steep ice all came more

*Making an ascent on Grosshorn* (Rob Collister).

themselves, as rock climbers. Rob Smith's ascent of the Fiescherwand and occasional ascents of the Triolet North face were exceptions that proved the rule. The Dolomites were almost as popular a venue as Chamonix for an Alpine season. In that respect, Rob and I were different. Rob actively preferred ice to rock, while I have always enjoyed rock climbing but am not particularly gifted. On the other hand, week-long sojourns in the CIC hut had made us efficient ice climbers. Nevertheless, looking back, I am still surprised at our temerity in attempting the Grosshorn. Rob was well-versed in Alpine lore, but in my case I am sure that ignorance was bliss. I had never heard of Welzenbach and was quite unaware of the reputation his climbs had acquired, which was a great advantage. The difficulty of a climb can often lie in the head as much as in the configuration of rock or ice. I once retreated off the Central Pillar of Freney, in perfect weather, and have regretted it ever since. Ostensibly, we were stopped fairly low down by a pitch we just could not climb. In retrospect I think I was simply fazed by having read Bonatti's account of the harrowing and tragic retreat from that place. My partner, the imperturbable Dick Renshaw, would undoubtedly have worried away until he found a way up or round that pitch, but I was too aware of how high and remote we were, too affected by the historical aura of the place. If reading books can add depth and resonance to the immediate sensations of climbing, it can also make individual climbs much harder. The Eiger with its gruesome, morbidly-documented history, is an extreme example. Even Bonatti failed here to assert mind over matter and retreated from his one solo attempt.

The other difficulty with big Alpine climbs is their appearance. Looked at from straight on, a 50° ice face appears vertical, a rock wall seems sheer and featureless. Experience tells you that ice slopes are rarely as steep as they look, and that close inspection will reveal cracks and flaws in the most compact piece of rock. But it still takes a mental effort, a deliberate stifling of the imagination, first to approach the very foot of a big climb, then to ignore the awful scale of the thing, 1,000 m or more stretching endlessly above and concentrate on the moves in front of your nose, or at most the line of the next pitch. The need to start as early as midnight to ensure well frozen snow and to reduce the danger from stones or series, is a

naturally. After a fortnight in the Bernina Alps, Rob Ferguson and I felt confident enough to attempt our first *grande course*. We chose the north face of the Grosshorn, an ice climb on the Lauterbrunnen Wall. At that time most major ice routes in the Alps had received very few ascents, and even fewer by British parties. Ice axes with curved or drooped picks had not yet appeared on the market and protection was provided either by long pegs that had to be laboriously chopped out of the ice after use or by ice screws that were more suitable for opening wine bottles than for holding a fall. Everyone talked about front-pointing, but nobody practised it, except on neve. Rob and I had tried to front-point the Scersen Eisnase After 30 ft, discretion proved the better part of valour and we compromised by cutting bucket steps into which we mantleshelfed. British climbers were regarded, and regarded

great help in this respect. One can be well up a face before day breaks, with no need to contemplate it from a distance. In the case of the Grosshorn we were helped even further by a layer of low cloud which, if unpromising for the morrow, at least hid the face from view on our walk up to the Schmadri hut.

Already ensconced in the hut, in fact the only people there, were two other Brits, Dennis Davis and Ray College. We had come to climb one route of several on the Lanterbrunnen Wall, none of which had received a British ascent and yet here was another British party attempting exactly the same route on the same day. We were rather overawed to be in such company; Dennis was a veteran of several Himalayan expeditions and the previous year Ray had climbed The Pear, The Walker and The Eiger in the space of a two-week holiday. They were welcoming and quite uncondescending, however, and we agreed to join forces next day.

After the usual uncommunicative candle-lit breakfast, 'each dwelling all to himself in the hermitage of his own mind', we left the hut some time in the small hours, picked a sleepy way over moraines, cramponed up some neves; and crossed the bergschrund; always a

**Above** *The north face of Grosshorn* (Rob Collister).

**Above right** *North face of Grosshorn* (Rob Collister).

**Right** *A spectacular Alpine dawn* (Rob Collister).

mental Rubicon, without difficulty. At dawn we were moving together up steepening snow slopes. Shortly afterwards the three of us were belayed to a single tied-off corkscrew, anxiously watching Ray as he methodically chopped his way through the narrows formed by two rock buttresses, on ice only a couple of inches thick. Above stretched 1,500 ft of hard ice, demanding steps all the way. As the day wore on we were glad to be four, to share the hard graft of cutting. When not taking our turn at the face, we shifted our weight from one leg to another on small stances, and contemplated the huge sweep of ice above, below and all around, feeling very small and vulnerable. Once, a sudden hostile whir made us glance round in time to see a single boulder from the upper cliffs bound past a few feet away. It was enough to keep me peering upwards from beneath my helmet, like an anxious tortoise, for the rest of the day. Another cause of

uneasiness was the weather. Great clouds were swirling below and sometimes about us. But, fortunately, they never developed into anything serious, and at evening the sky cleared.

Slowly, we chopped our way upwards. As we rose, the sun dropped. The last few hundred feet seemed harder and steeper, interminable; perhaps we were just growing tired. When dark fell, we were still well below the summit but there was no incentive to stop, and we continued doggedly by torch light. My mind was wandering now, feet were cold, legs stiff and aching. It was 10 pm before we finally emerged on to the top. We had been climbing 21 hours, climbing characterized more by nervous tension than any actual difficulty. I was aware of chains of light down in the valley. It was 1 August, a Swiss national holiday when children carrying lanterns process through the villages. Our head-torches, we learned later, were taken to be a part of the celebrations. I think the others brewed up; I was too tired to bother. Pulling on my duvet and cagoule, I put my feet into my rucksack, sat on the rope, and fell asleep in a sitting position among some rocks.

There can be few sports in which the distinction between pleasure and happiness is so marked as it is in climbing, particularly climbing in big mountains. Moments of conscious pleasure during the day had been few, moments of discomfort legion. From the torch flashed into my eyes at midnight to the agonising cramp in my calves during that bivouac, there had been suffering of one sort or another. Indigestion, cold, heat, thirst, fatigue and fear had been the dominant sensations of the day. Yet, at the end of it, I was indisputably happy. It was not just relief at a task accomplished, satisfaction at an ambition achieved or anticipation of a limited acclaim. Born of those hours of fatigue, deprivation and stress, in which beauty and grandeur were absorbed almost subliminally, grew an inward singing, which would linger on as a calm content for weeks afterwards. Feelings of regret, sadness, disappointment, seem to be common among mountaineers writing about summit moments, but I have never experienced them. Perhaps my climbs have never been hard enough, or been planned and dreamed about for long enough. All I know is that a taxing Alpine climb leaves me feeling positive about life in general for a long time

afterwards. Surely, that is why most of us climb mountains? But there are degrees of happiness. As in so many spheres, the reward is in proportion to the effort expended. In climbing terms, it was some time before I experienced again quite the same high I felt when we awoke to a clear sunny morning on top of the Grosshorn.

Back in the Alps two years later, ice faces seemed suddenly almost straightforward, and everyone was climbing them. Both Chouinard and Saleva were producing axes and hammers with curved picks, designed to penetrate ice rather than shatter it. With such weapons front-printing became a viable option on the hardest and steepest of ice. Ice climbs could be achieved in fast times even in unfavourable conditions of bare ice rather than neve, yet the leader could feel, and actually was, more

*Brenva face from low on Brenva Spur* (Rob Collister).

*Just after sunrise on the Brenva Spur, the rewards of an Alpine start* (Rob Collister).

secure than when simply standing in steps. Bivouacs, too, had become relatively comfortable with the appearance of the Karrimat. Closed-cell foam had been in use in the States for some years but it only became widely available in Britain after the Annapurna South Face expedition of 1970. In addition, I had acquired a two-man nylon Zdarski sack, and had decided that a lightweight sleeping bag made more sense than a down jacket weighing the same. Now, so long as we could find room to lie or sit, any bivouac could be a cosy affair.

After several weeks of climbing whenever the weather permitted, on both snow and rock, I found myself fit and confident but temporarily without a partner. I rather welcomed the opportunity to try some climbs on my own. I had few qualms about climbing solo, for a large proportion of all Alpine climbing is unroped or moving together. But to be totally alone on a long climb would be something quite new. I started with the Frendo Spur which went without incident, but there were so many other climbers scattered up and down the route that it did not feel like soloing at all. Next, I decided to try the Route Major

on the Brenva Face of Mont Blanc, a long, serious climb but not technically too difficult; and this time I found what I was looking for.

Travelling alone on glaciers is a hazardous business so I was glad to team up with a pair of Norwegians, bound for the Grand Capucin, for the journey across the Vallée Blanche from the Midi. The weather had been poor for some days and I was alone in the Trident hut that night until an Italian guide and his client arrived long after I had gone to bed. They were still asleep when I left just before 1 am, tip-toeing thunderously in crampons on the metal-walkway outside the hut. The moon was high and almost full, the torch unnecessary as I descended steeply on to the glacier and contoured between some big open crevasses. Col Moore was in shadow, steep and icy but covered with old steps. The Brenva face glowered hugely overhead, but I did not allow myself to contemplate its immensity or the lethal potential of those batteries of seracs up above, and set off on a long rising traverse into the face. At first, the climbing was messy and unpleasant, on loose debris left by a recent rock fall which had spilled down the face, like

**Right** *The Brenva Spur* (Rob Collister).

**Far right** *Upper Brenva face from Brenva Spur, with Great Couloir on the right, Pear Buttress to the left, and showing the major route between the two* (Rob Collister).

puke on a drunkard's chin I remember thinking. Once clear, it was a matter of keeping to the snow, zigzagging through the rock, gaining height but always traversing leftwards. Several times I had to climb down the vertical side of an avalanche runnel deeply scored into the mountain, and up the other side. Once I had to wait a full minute as a torrent of spindrift hissed past. Finally, I recognized the dark mass of the Sentinelle and climbing the chimney at its side emerged on the edge of the infamous Great Couloir, the main chute for avalanches from the upper regions of the face. I listened hard, took a deep breath, and literally ran across a hundred feet or so of hard but easy-angled water-ice. I did not pause until I had scrambled up rocks on the far side and was at last on the ridge crest

discerned 40 years before by Graham Brown as the safest line in a dangerous place. There, panting, I stopped and looked around. Way below on the Col Moore, two torches flickered as the Italians set off up the Brenva Spur. I felt separated from them not just by distance but by a gulf of nervous tension. Suddenly, I realized just how frightened I had been of that traverse beneath the seracs. Even in cold conditions, it smacks a little of Russian roulette. Now I found myself actively looking foward to the climbing ahead.

The rock on the spur was nowhere hard but often it was iced and always it demanded attention. The famous snow aretes came and went, the dark preventing a full appreciation of their position. Climbing in bare hands I was aware of the temperature dropping as I gained height and dawn approached. I was fit enough to move fast and continuously and I had to make a conscious effort to relax, to slow down and take in what was around me. I was possessed by a feverish impulse that urged me on, a reaction I suppose to being alone in the dark in such a place. Every now and then I forced myself to stop, to gaze across at the streak of light appearing behind the Diable ridge, the odd flashes of lightning over the Gran Paradiso, or the summit of the Aiguille Blanche where Rob and I had sat a few weeks before.

The buttress at the top of the spur was difficult. It was still dark enough to need a torch and the rock was steep. Had I a rope, I would have put it on. As it was, I made do with a long sling threaded through an *in situ* peg as I hauled myself over an ice-coated chock-stone. My first attempts in crampons were unsuccessful and, in the end, I had to take them off and use small incut holds on either side of the chimney. The problem was that I found myself then in an icy gully, in no position to refit the crampons. Acutely aware of 4,000 ft of Brenva face stretching away below, I cut steps with the utmost care until the ice ran out and I found myself tip-toeing reluctantly up a verglassed slab.

Now I was beneath the final serac wall recalling Bonatti's account of pegging up vertical ice. Seracs are never the same from one year to the next, however, and sure enough there was a way through in which only a short traverse was steep. Above, it was all plain sailing, if hard work through crusted powder. I was glad to find some old tracks which made life easier, and plodded upwards into the dawning day, exulting inwardly if not outwardly. Little more than five hours after leaving the hut, and at the very moment that the sun rose above the horizon, I reached the summit. I pulled on a windproof and sat on my sack to look over valleys filled with blue haze to the Vertes and the Jorasses; and beyond to the Grand Combin and the distant peaks of the Valais. I strove to encompass it all and imprint the moment on my memory. Yet I can recall no other details of that view now. It is always the same. It is incidents and random impressions from the ascent that stick in the mind. The views and spectacular surroundings, wonderful though they can be, become merely the matrix for a climb. I always marvel at the descriptions of W. H. Murray and Geoffrey Winthrop Young; they must have trained themselves to be verbal photographers of their surroundings. Yet I do not really regret such

failures of memory, or that I took no camera with me that day. For what I do remember is the stillness and inner quiet of those moments, a glimpse of an enviable state of being, all too easily dispelled by the usual chatter of consciousness when one starts fiddling with a camera or writing in a note-book.

Two figures appeared at the other end of the long summit crest. It was time to go. Bubbling with *joie de vivre*, grateful for those few minutes to myself I ran down the mountainside passed a long, long caravan of despairing, ashen-faced climbers stuggling with the altitude. Revelling in health and youth and a comfortable pair of boots, I scorned railway and telepherique, and by 10.30 am was strolling through Chaminox eating peaches, utterly content, as the clouds of a freak storm swept violently over Mont Blanc.

After that year my Alpine activities diversified. No longer was I constrained by the summer season. There was the pristine purity of the Alps in mid-winter to experience. A whole new world of delight opened up when I skied the High Level Route in Spring. I discovered that Alpinism could be practised beyond the Alps and that mountain exploration could be as satisfying as reaching summits. Summer climbs in the Alps tended to be really memorable only when things went wrong, being caught out by bad weather, for instance, or dropping my axe in the middle of a difficult face. One exception, however, was when, almost by accident, Geoff Cohen and I did a new route.

Our intention had been to climb the Boivin-Vallencant route on the Nant Blanc face of the Aiguille-Sans Nom (itself really just a shoulder of the Vertes); but as we descended towards the glacier from the Grands Montets, we noticed a thin but continuous white ribbon running through the upper rocks of the face and well to the left of Boivin-Vallencant line. After a comfortable bivouac beside the glacier, in twelve exhilarating hours we climbed a straightforward buttress at the bottom of the face, moved together on perfect snow-ice up the central ice-field, and weaved a way on ice of a Scottish character through steep rock at the top, never quite sure where the next pitch would take us. It felt a fine climb, safe from objective dangers and not easy, though I have never heard of anyone bothering to repeat it. In the words of Dave Roberts after a first ascent on Mount Dickey: 'The joy that so eludes our everyday affairs was there in abundance: we had done exactly what we set out to do'. But the best was yet to come. Beneath us, as we traversed the delicate Sans Nom ridge to the summit of the Verte, the valleys were filled with cloud, rising, falling, seething, breaking, no mere cotton-wool carpet but as mobile and ever changing as the sea. We took our time, pausing to gaze around, lingering on the top. Why hurry down to a stuffy over-crowded hut on such an evening? We bivouacked again halfway down the Grande Rocheuse with a wide-angled view from the alpenglow on Mont Blanc across to the Jorasses, jutting out of the cloud like a rock above a foam of ruddy gold, and on to the dissolving blues, greys, purples and violets in the East over the Triolet. The sun was finally fading from the tops when, suddenly, the shadow of the Verte appeared on the cloud below us, a gigantic cone stretching to the horizon. As the stars came out and night crept over us, we lay silent and wide-awake on our respective ledges, reluctant to let the day pass into memory.

Rob Collister is married with three children and lives in North Wales where he works as a self-employed guide. He is a member of ABMC. He read history, English and mountaineering at Cambridge University. He first visited the Alps in 1967 and since then has been back at least once a year. He has also taken part in a dozen lightweight expeditions to different parts of the Himalayas, as well as climbs and ski journeys in Antarctica, Greenland, Alaska, South America and Kenya.

# September: Climbing in New England

## JILL LAWRENCE

New England in the Eastern United States might seem a strange place to come in search of rockclimbing. The larger towns and cities, predominated by flatness; concrete; hoardings and parking lots do not give one a sense of the outdoors or openness; on the contrary they are quite claustrophobic. However, venturing away from the cities the landscape changes rapidly, from artificial colours and forms to more natural ones. Green is the predominant colour in summer, and everywhere there are trees, leaving very few open spaces. Within the mass of greenery covering New England there is very little exposed rock suitable for climbing. However, hidden away amidst the vegetation, jewels are revealed that earlier climbers have discovered, then polished, to provide amazing playgrounds to which climbers from all over the world make a pilgrimage, too. The two major areas are Cathedral Cliffs situated in New Hampshire, and the Shawangunks in New York state. September and October are considered the best months to climb there. Fall, as Americans term autumn, is felt to have the optimum weather conditions.

In 1983 I was fortunate enough to have all of the autumn available to climb. I had spent the summer hot and sweaty, working at a summer school outside Boston, where often the humidity was around 80 per cent. The climbing plan was to spend the early part of September in North Conway at Cathedral, then as the weather cooled move south to spend the second half of September in the Gunks. Fortunately for me my climbing partner, Rosie Andrews, was familiar with both areas. Rosie had actually worked for a climbing school in North Conway, and she had also spent a lot of her earlier climbing career pushing her standard up the grades on Gunks overhangs. Having a partner with both knowledge of the areas and social contacts meant I was set up for an exciting climbing trip.

The decision to make North Conway our first venue was made because it is a good

distance north of the Gunks, around 250 miles, and consequently winter comes much earlier. The climbing season in New Hampshire is really quite a short one. The winters are long and cold, often providing great ice climbing conditions. Spring is usually very wet, whilst the summer months can be too hot and humid. They are accompanied by swarms of nasty bugs that take great delight from biting and sucking blood from any flesh they can get their teeth into. In September the weather is at its best, when cooler, clearer air predominates. This is generally more stable giving rise to fewer thunderstorms. The other bonus at this time of year is the trees. The leaves change to give a spectacular display of colour, blending from yellow through orange then into the deep reds of maples. The whole effect quite surpasses even the very best autumn colours I can ever remember at home. The colour change is a large tourist attraction, with newspapers predicting the optimum weekends for viewing. Whole coachloads of 'leaf peepers' can be seen emerging then disappearing into the foliage, armed with an impressive array of cameras. The fall colours give a softness, variety and depth to the landscape that is missing in summer when green predominates.

Rosie and I set out north from Boston on interstate highway 93, we left 93 just past Laconia taking 25, then 16, north into the White Mountains, and continued towards the small town of North Conway. There was a sense of *déjà vu* driving along the highway. Names were so familiar, evoking memories of rural and urban England; Manchester, Dover, Bristol, and Peterborough exits flashed in front of my eyes. Once we left the highway there were splendid lakes, varying in size from a mile long, to Lake Winnipesaukee that was 30 miles in length. They were splendid, shiny, blue-grey expanses that sparkled and glistened in the morning light. Soon we were nearing North Conway. From here it was only a couple of miles to Cathedral Ledges and the climbing

**Above** *Pitch 2 traverse on Bonnie's Roof* (Alison Watt).

**Right** *Bonnie's Roof on Trapps Gunks. Climber Mandy Glanville* (Gill Price).

we had come to do. It was early afternoon when we arrived so there was time to view the cliff and do a route.

The rock is excellent granite with a diversity of angles giving a variety of slabs, walls and overhangs. At the central point the cliffs are 500 ft high and offer continuous steep faces. To the left the lines are broken by ledges and trees, and on the right too the verticality is split by ledges offering escape routes. For me this did not detract from the climbing as it facilitated the combining of different pitches of several routes to give quality climbing at whatever standard one desired. Approaches to the routes were short, the rock was solid, with excellent protection, and overall I was anticipating having a good time. There were further delights; to the left of Cathedral there is a large sweep of slabs called Whitehorse Ledges, which give the finest slab climbing available on the East coast.

For today our attention was to be focused on Cathedral. Funhouse, a three star 5.7 was

**Left** *Climber Gill Price tackles Krapps Last Tape, S.10, Skytop Gunks* (Mandy Glanville).

**Left** *Rosie Andrews on Stannards Roof. 5.a. Lost City Gunks* (Jill Lawrence).

our choice. By climbing this with Black Lung and Final Gesture, also 5.7, we would get four pitches at about severe standard. We hoped this would give a gentle introduction to the rock, since after ten weeks of no climbing we were more than prepared to be cautious. The route had tremendous variety, bridging and lay-backing on the first pitch, face climbing on a steep slab for the second, quite strenuous jamming on the third pitch, with an awkward overhanging crack to finish. At the top there were easy slabs that brought us to the woods where numerous paths enticed us into their leafy shade. Choosing one we arrived at the tourist lookout, from where the view was excellent. The saco valley was below, with the line of the river evident more from the gap in the vegetation than from a clear view of the water. Echo Lake was sparkling in the sunlight, where miniature figures swam and boated on its shiny surface. This was also a good spot to view the upper wall, prominent on this is tourist treat, at that time still graded 5.10 A2. The local hot-shot climbers of the area had reputedly been working hard to be the first to free this. I heard it was finally done some time in 1985 by Lynn Hill; and given 5.12. Following another path the road was soon in view, revealing a one-and-a-half-mile walk downhill to the base. The spectacle of someone bedecked in climbing paraphernalia with her thumb out seemed to ensure a ride back down to the base.

Rosie had contacted Paul Ross, once an aficionado of the Lake District where he had been involved in many first ascents; now he was playing land baron just outside North Conway. We were to camp in his garden. Garden is not exactly the right word; yes, there was an area with some flowers, and a dog pen full of yapping Yorkshire terriers, which Paul bred. The dogs were noisy but not nearly as ferocious as the geese running around the yard, which were apt to charge anything that moved accompanied by the most horrifying screeching. But there were also several acres of land covered in trees that sloped steeply, flattening out right on the bank of the river. It was here next to the river that we were to camp. The spot was perfect, quiet and private, with its very own swimming spot. At night the sound of the wind in the trees and water in the river combined to sing us to sleep with their magical lullabies.

The mornings were wonderful, the way the light slanted through the trees, dancing and dappling on the leaves, creating mystical shadows on the water, shifting and changing to create new shapes, as the sun rose higher. I had always been a little wary of people who expounded the outwardbound delights of 'run and dip', which had seemed a little too hearty for my delicate morning constitution. Nonetheless after two days Rosie and I had acquired the habit of getting up at 6.30, going for a short, three-mile run, then plunging into the cool, rapid current of the river. Not only did we maintain this during our stay, we delighted in it, feeling deprived once we moved on from New Hampshire.

The next day we decided to try something a little harder. The choice was The Book of Solemnity, a three star route rated 5.10. Although there was a good chance it might prove to be too ambitious, we did an excellent job of convincing each other that we should not be under-achieving. In favour of this Rosie knew it was well protected. The line was a good one, a two-pitch, clean-looking corner with a roof at half height. I took the first pitch, and everything was fine until the roof; where small polished face holds beckoned me rightwards in order to avoid the roof. After a lot of hesitation accompanied by much back and forth, I finally moved across, convinced I would fall. I made it safely to the belay instead. Rosie was quickly at my side, seemingly floating over the section where I had my difficulties. On her lead it was somewhat gratifying to see she hesitated where the corner ended trying to decide whether to go high or low to reach better holds and the belay. My attempt to appear as if I was floating effortlessly up the pitch was short-lived, my nonchalance turned to the 'keep it tight routine', as my foot refused to stick to a crystal nubbin that was the key to moving left.

Whilst we were climbing the sky had clouded over and the first drops of rain fell. Using Upper Refuge, described in the guide as a delightful 5.5 face climb we headed for the summit. Delightful for the first pitch, yes, but by the final pitch it was too exciting. The rain was now heavy, the rock was wet, making us thankful for the numerous nut placements. Reaching the road, naturally there was not a car in sight. It was a squelchy, soggy pair who reached Rosie's car at the bottom, then headed for the nearest coffee shop. The one we found had great blueberry muffins, a sort of individual sponge cake full of fruit. Here we sat and steamed, drinking endless refills of coffee until it stopped raining.

Deciding it was too late to do another route we headed for IME, one of the local climbing shops, not with the intention of buying anything, but to exchange gossip, talk about our day and ask other climbers about theirs. The shop was busy. The talk was of the new consignment of rock boots that had just arrived. Firés were just starting to be imported into the States at that point and whilst there were lots of claims going around about the superiority of the boots few people had actually tried them out. Hence their validity as the stickiest thing since super glue was still untested. Nonetheless Rosie and I tried on a pair, cramming our feet sockless into the smallest shoes we could, having been warned that they stretched a lot. They were expensive so we took time to think about it before making a decision. That night we met Doug Madara, a local guide. He had been using the boots for the past three months and sang their praises. Next day we were first in the shop impatient to spend some of the dollars we had earned in the summer.

Our venue for the new boot trial was to be Whitehorse ledges on a 5.9 called Children's Crusade. If the boots felt OK Rosie was keen to attempt the direct finish graded 5.11. With some trepidation I set off up the leftward trending, unprotected, 5.7 dike, until it was possible to traverse right then continue up the dike to the belay. At some point there was a bolt for protection and I was thankful for it as I was feeling somewhat dubious in my new footwear. Looking up at the second pitch it was hard to see any holds or any protection. Nonetheless Rosie led it steadily, calmly sorting out the best foot position, the best handhold combination. Although the holds were small they turned out to be sharp and positive, this was encouraging and served to entice Rosie upwards between the sparce fixed protection. It was a delightful pitch to follow, holds appearing just when they were needed, yet technical enough to require careful combinations of moves, all without having to worry about the runouts between gear. I led the easier face pitch and crack above which brought us to the bottom of the direct finish. Rosie was feeling good in her new Firés so was ready to try the direct. It looked steep but not too long. There was a shallow corner with a small overhang above it then a very steep looking corner higher up.

'Shit! This is strenuous!' floated down to me, Rosie was combining layback then bridging moves on the steep corner above. Her footwork looked intricate, requiring constant repositioning and shifts of her body weight, each sequence of movement resulted in only a few inches of height gained. My neck was getting stiff, my hands were constantly taking in or paying out the double ropes we were using. Slowly but surely Rosie got smaller until she disappeared, then shouted 'Off belay'. We were both relieved and excited. Rosie could now relax completely, whereas I was rather apprehensively heading off towards the steepness. Now I understood the foot switches, my calves aching from the wide bridging meant that constant movement was required to relieve the slow burn towards cramp. The position on the final overhanging section of the corner was impressive to say the least. Glancing down the rock was on the periphery of my vision, the main view was space, a lot of it! We hugged, smiling and congratulating each other on the first 5.11 of the season. The vote was ten out of ten for the new Firés.

Although both of us acknowledge that we climb for fun there is 'work fun' and 'play fun'. The direct finish was more in the category of 'work fun', so we felt quite justified in heading for the river and wallowing in the cool water. There was a spot where it was possible to do stationary swimming for miles if one wished. The current was strong enough to swim against and remain completely still. However, a momentary lapse in rhythm sent one spinning off down stream with a real struggle to regain a stable position. Finally exhausted we headed back to the camp site. It felt good and elating though, that tiredness that comes from pushing oneself and succeeding. It is a satisfied, relaxed, almost sensual feeling, muscles aching slightly and limbs heavy from the day's efforts.

Inspired by Rosie's example I wanted to try a 5.11 lead, and was recommended Airation, a classic-looking finger crack that was reputed to be strenuous. Airation is on the upper wall at Cathedral, so in order to reach the start we opted to solo up Thin Air, a classic 5.6. There was a party on the route, which is deservedly popular, but fortunately they were kind enough to let us pass. The second pitch was exceptionally good value for its grade,

*Short pitch up to a ledge below Double Issima* (Jill Lawrence).

consisting of a long traverse to the right on small holds. For someone who was just leading 5.6 it would present a challenging lead as the protection is only just adequate. Soloing it felt quite exciting.

Airation was above us. The line was elegant; it started with a wider crack that soon narrowed. Then after a small pod there was a thinner crack that looked absolutely vertical and was about finger size. From the ground there were no holds visible on the wall, but the crack looked like it would protect well. I had a half size friend that I planned to save for a quick placement near the top having been warned it was a disaster to hang around too long at that point. The very best of intentions sometimes get forgotten, so there I was on the upper crack willing my fingers to stay in the finger locks while I zealously placed far too many runners. It was steep, with only tiny footholds. I did think I would fall off, and I was scared of that, too scared to be bold and just blast the thing. Somehow I had enough strength to get in four good runners, then the

half size friend at the top, all in about 20 ft of crack. My workout on the pegboard, cranking and locking off on one arm for the summer were paying off; Yes; I was using twice as much energy as I needed but nonetheless I was getting up the route without falling. Another move on a not so great finger lock allowed me to reach high to a perfect one, footholds appeared and the difficulties were over. Panting and sweating, still trembling slightly from the adrenalin coursing through my body, I belayed to a large tree and could tell a very large grin was taking over my face. Rosie cursed me a little as she fiddled with my well-placed protection, finally leaving one very stuck wire in to be retrieved on abseil. It didn't mar our jubilation and we felt good about our climbing and wanted to test ourselves on something longer and more sustained before leaving New Hampshire. The obvious choice was to do a route on Cannon Cliff.

Cannon Mountain is 4,077 ft high and Cannon Cliff is on its east face. At its highest the cliff is 1,000 ft and offers a variety of climbs. Short one pitch routes, long and difficult free climbs, even big wall aid routes requiring overnight bivouacs. The rock is granite, but because of the extreme weather conditions in winter, it is like alpine rock, that is occasionally loose and prone to exfoliation. Consequently, the routes are serious undertakings. Additionally bad weather arrives from the west and can take climbers completely by surprise at any point on a long route. The route we wanted to do, VMC Direct Direct was a popular one, so we hoped it would be quite solid. Altogether it would provide nine pitches of climbing, to include four 5.10 pitches and one 5.9 pitch, a fitting finale to our stay in New Hampshire.

The drive over to Franconia Notch was quite beautiful. From North Conway we took the Kangamangus Highway, which wound its way across the White Mountains. The mountains looked wild and unspoilt, with the autumn colours looking splendid in the soft morning light. Soon we were parking at Boise rock, then heading up into the trees towards the talus slope. It was a hot steep scramble up this and then a final thrash through bushes before the base of the cliff. The start of the route was easy to find, the well worn path testifying to its popularity. Above, a line of obvious corners clearly marked the first four pitches of the route. The first hard pitch was superb climbing. A combination of lay-backing and bridging was needed to overcome the difficulties in the steep corner. The crack was good making protection, particularly friends, easy to place. At the roof it was necessary to traverse right on underclings to regain the continuation of the corner. By this time my arms were pretty pumped, the holds were good but it was steep. Thankfully I reached the belay, having put 140 ft of exciting climbing below me. There was another corner above with yet another overhang. Originally the route had aided directly over the roof, then up, before heading right on bolts to reach the belay. The free version traversed right under the overhang, then followed a corner to the belay. Pitch four went fast a combination of face and corner climbing at 5.9; we were moving well and making good time.

Rosie set off on the fifth pitch, suddenly she was back down at the belay with me, faster than either of us had expected. The first 10 ft off the belay was a boulder problem with no protection. It was a very steep slab needing

good friction technique and the ability to crank on very small crystals. Admittedly Rosie had both of these, but nonetheless it took a few tries before she made it. At each try I thought there was a real danger of her landing on my head and could not decide which was best, to try to catch her or to move out of the way. We both agreed it seemed harder than its 5.10 rating. The pitch above that brought us on to a large ledge, with a recess at the back, almost a shallow cave. This feature on the face was known as the 'cow's mouth', although we could never figure out how it had acquired that name. The pitch above was the final 5.10 before the route eased off to easy slabs to finish. The guidebook description said, 'Struggle past the overhang', and that was exactly what we did — struggle! The holds were poor, we were tired, and it was very overhanging.

Scrambling around the top of the cliff we headed for the group of rocks known as The Old Man. When these are viewed from Profile Lake below, with a touch of imagination they do look like a person's face in profile. It was a surprise on reaching them to see that they were held together with concrete complete with concrete runnels to drain the water away. Apparently The Old Man was falling down, the reinforcing was necessary if it was to remain as a tourist attraction. The descent was down to Profile Lake via a well-worn trail. It felt like a long way, but this was more a reflection of our tired state than the actual distance. Once down at the lake there was an excellent view of The Old Man. Back at the car we could see the cliff but it was now in shadow. However, it was possible to make out the line of the route. Contemplating it from below was a satisfying feeling. It had been a fine finale to our stay in New Hampshire. Now we felt ready for a couple of days' rest before heading south to the Shawangunks.

The Gunks as they are known almost universally are situated about 7 miles outside of the small town of New Paltz in New York State. From New Paltz the white line of the cliffs stands out from the predominating greenery to show a white line that must be about three miles in length. The cliffs were first discovered in 1935 by Fritz Wieser. With a small group of friends he was able to leisurely pick out lines on the cliff and slowly develop the area.

Today a leisurely pace for any of the classic

routes, particularly on a weekend, would mean queuing. The Gunks are about 90 miles from New York City and about 120 miles from New Jersey. Each week-end hundreds of climbers descend into the Mohonk Trust Reserve to festoon the rocks with criss-crossing ropes and more recently, psychedelic tights. The major cliffs are all on the preserve land; a non-profit organization set up in 1963 in order to preserve 5,000 acres of open land. There is no problem over access for climbers, they are in fact welcomed. However, a small user fee is charged in the form of a day, week or season permit. To myself coming from Britain it seemed an anathema to be paying for the right to use a climbing area and I was fully prepared to avoid the fee collecting ranger. However, I quickly realized that 99 per cent of the climbers, hot-shots and beginners alike, were all happy to contribute to preserving the land, in order that it continue to be available for themselves and future generations, as a rural area providing adventure, challenge and escape from the city.

Relationships between climbers and rangers were excellent. The place was clean, there was almost no litter, climbers seemed to make a conscious commitment to preserving the environment; and after weekends the rangers would do a clean up, removing any stray trash. As a consequence of talking to local climbers and the rangers, I was soon convinced, and sported a permit button.

It is amazing how different areas have their own particular style of climbing, and this seems to be particularly true of the USA. In Yosemite it is long cracks with jam after jam, in Toulomn meadows it is faith in friction and a good head for runouts, in the Gunks it is the ability to crank hard on your fingers on overhanging rock. The rock is laid in bands of horizontal strata; it is a form of conglomorate on a bed of shale. The colours are reminiscent of limestone, showing white through grey into yellow. From a distance the rock does not look very appealing and one might be tempted to dismiss it as a 'heap of choss'. However, closer inspection reveals the rock to be very solid. Although there are very few aesthetic natural lines, there are endless possibilities for eliminates, straight up, overhangs, roofs, then more roofs to the top. Holds are almost always horizontal finger pulls; how much of one's hand or finger can be placed on the hold will dictate the difficulty. Originally many of the

routes were pegged, a number of old rusty pitons remain in routes, generally these are not to be trusted and it is wise to back them up if at all possible.

The horizontal cracks are perfect for placing friends, although it is prudent to place perlon on the stalk so they can be tied off to give a shorter stem thus reducing the leverage on the stalk. (Gunks climbers like to use kevlar for this; the 5 mm size is as strong as steel cable.) For the harder routes small brass nuts or the newer steel ones seem to nicely wedge themselves in delicate little cracks and fractures. Generally routes are so steep at all grades that there is little danger of hitting anything if one falls.

Driving out of New Paltz on 299, the road eventually winds its way uphill towards the

**Left** *Pitch 2, Birdie Party* (Alison Watt).

cliff, and it is possible to park. To the left of the road are the Near Trapps, and the footpath that continues out to Bayards and Millbrook cliffs; to the right are the Trapps and access to Skytop. The access around the Trust, is on old carriage roads that are utilized as footpaths. They are a reminder of a bygone era when access to the area was the privilege of a small moneyed elite. Today climbers and hikers use their leafy shade to either get to routes, or to view the estate. Walking towards the Trapps it is necessary to pass below the Uberfall, always a crowded spot. Here the rangers sell permits, and climbers congregate to gossip and exchange information about climbs. Always there is someone miming a sequence of moves they thought were either desperate, or a 'cinch'. Here too, partners can be found for

the day; the notice board announces gear for sale, and rides to every part of the U.S. 'share gas'. It is a good spot for hanging out, with entertainment laid on; there are generally people bouldering, and fancy tights and chalk bags fly through the air with amazing regularity.

Rosie and I had camped at the small sight just before the Near Trapps. Although it was near the road it was quiet, midweek, although the week-end could be a rowdy time. People would arrive right through the night and they seemed to have the strange idea that if they are in their tents and can't see out, the noise can't get out either. Nonetheless the advantages of camping there outweighed the disadvantages; we were right there at the cliff, no driving was needed, the carriage roads were excellent for running on, they were away from traffic and provided scope for great circuits and there was water and toilets (although unfortunately no showers). The disadvantages were, that the city dwellers would screech in late on a Friday night, stereos blaring, car doors banging, beer cans popping. However, come Sunday they were gone, and once again it became possible to lie in the tent and hear both the wind high in the tree tops, and small animals snuffling around for food whilst we talked in whispers in order not to disturb the calm of the woods.

After our success in New Hampshire we were enthusiastic to start climbing. Rosie suggested, 'Try something reasonable first, see how you like the rock'. This turned out to be excellent advice. Getting on the rock it was a shock to realize how steep and strenuous most of the routes were, and this made the majority of them quite intimidating propositions. The routes were such that often it was necessary to do a series of moves to pass overhangs, leaving protection behind, out of sight below the overhangs, with no certainty of being able to get a piece in above.

We started our Gunks climbing on Bonnies Roof, a classic 5.9. This is an impressive looking corner, steep and capped by very large-looking overhangs. The corner went pretty easily, and a combination of lay-back and bridging moves soon brought one to below the roof. The corner certainly had been steep, but the holds were good jugs that gave one a nice secure feeling, while the belay was impressively situated below the large overhangs. The second pitch traversed out left on small delicate holds, to gain an edge that was climbed to the summit, thus avoiding the horrendous-looking overhangs that were bristling above. The position on the traverse was exposed, a complete contrast to the jug pulling security below. This pitch brought us to a large ledge that ran right across the face, from where it was possible to traverse the face easily, and gain the descent route. This was a reverse of Silly Chimney, a 5.1; that saved us continuing up the poor quality rock above.

To the left of Bonnies Roof was Antsline, another splendid-looking corner. The start was very steep, so I was quickly into that cycle of putting in protection because it was steep and strenuous. This of course got my arms pumped, which made me place more protection as I became more convinced that I would fall; a cycle that is so tough to break

once started! Logically when it occurs part of me remains rational and knows its completely irrational behaviour. However, intervention always feels so difficult and the irrational tends to reign supreme. The outcome was my arrival at the belay, hot, panting and sweating, wondering if I would have enough strength to tie into the belay. The lessons to be learnt were that Gunks climbing is best done quickly, moves sorted out well in advance, and that boldness in protection placement is more conducive to success on a pitch. However, ideals are one thing; reality still found me putting in lots of pro once a route started to feel steep and strenuous. (I wonder if it really is possible to train oneself to be bolder. Obviously as strength and stamina improve one becomes more prepared to leave gear behind, but does the actuality of the risk remain proportionately the same?) The

*Pitch 1, Bonnie's Roof* (Alison Watt).

experience on Antsline was enough to encourage me to remain working on 5.9s or easy 10s for a while.

Over the next few days life took on a familiar routine. Even with a leisurely start we would generally be ready to begin a route by 9.30; if it was at the Trapps, or Near Trapps, when our destination was Skytop it would be 10.30 before we started. Skytop is approximately a five-mile walk from the Uberfall along the carriage track which gives excellent views of the surrounding countryside. The path runs below the Trapps, making it useful for pinpointing the location of routes. Occasionally the rangers passed in their jeep and, if they had room, would offer a ride.

Skytop is owned by the Mohonk resort, which has the Mountain House Hotel on the property. It was first established in 1869, and is still flourishing today. The setting is quite beautiful. The hotel nestles in amongst the trees overlooking a lake to the front, with a green sweep of golf course behind. There are numerous trails through the woods, over the top of, and below Skytop itself, there are gazebos along the way at strategic points, to give not only shade and rest, but also splendid views. Climbing there at the weekend brings endless questions from passing tourists; 'How do you get the ropes to the top?' 'Don't you get scared?' 'I didn't realize women went climbing too'. Depending on one's tolerance level it was possible to give a variety of answers that either totally enlightened the viewers, or completely mystified them.

The rock at Skytop is excellent, very white and clean-looking, and it provides excellent climbing. The famous climb Foops is here, looking just as spectacular and intimidating as it did when it first appeared on the front cover of *Mountain*. It is a very, very big roof and no matter how many times I was told about the combination of holds and moves required to do the climb, my feet remained firmly on the ground beneath it, the prospect of the large roof just too intimidating for me. The routes I did do, however, were absolutely first rate and included: Mellow Yellow, a steep technical corner at 5.10 and Krapps last tape, 5.10, again steep but better protected. These two are both at the easier end of the 5.10 range. For the more adventurous, Half Assid, 5.10 +, a very thin crack (take lots of RPs) and Reign of Terror, 5.10 +, a steep crack with poor holds, provide excellent scarey diversions.

It was the last week in September, the nights were getting longer and cooler, the days were still brilliant. There were days when we would run after climbing, our loop basically circling the Trapps gave a splendid view of the sunset. Often there were clouds, probably New York State pollution, and these would be shot through with reds, golds, orange and yellows, breathtaking in their combinations of colours behind the changing autumn display of the treetops.

The coolness of the evenings and their length encouraged us to while away an occasional evening in the town. Two spots were the favourite haunts of climbers. One was the pavement outside 'David's Cookies', (the warm evening venue). Inside an amazingly sickly combination of rich creamy ice-cream could be purchased sandwiched between two large, sweet, chocolate chip cookies, for the

*A spectacular manoeuvre, Route Foops 5.11 around Skytop Gunks* (Dick Williams).

price of $2. This was definitely the place to avoid if one was attempting to remain on a low cholesterol diet as the myriad of flavours, and the smell of baking cookies was enough to tempt the most stalwart from their brown rice and vegetables. The second spot, affectionately known as, 'the time erazor'; I never got to know the real name of this family-run Italian restaurant situated on the main street, but it was a must for cold evenings as inside the atmosphere and temperature were warm and cozy. The reason for the name became apparent over time, it took ages to order, get served, eat and then get the bill. The whole process could take as long as three hours! One reason for this was that all the food was freshly baked on the premises; the other was there were only two waitresses who had to run around dealing with requests from over 30 customers. Notwithstanding all this, the food was good, the calzones and the pizzas with 'Sicillian crusts', seemed to come in only one size, large. Apart from these two venues New Paltz wasn't exactly a lively social scene. There were a few bars, but American climbers don't go in for the 'pub scene' like the British, preferring to sit in camp and drink beer and talk, or they go to bed early.

During our stay we had visited most of the cliffs, although there was another cliff we wanted to visit before our trip ended, Lost City. This cliff is set back in the woods behind the Trapps, and is not very often frequented. One of the reasons for this has been the deliberate exclusion of this area from the guidebook. I am not exactly sure of the rationale behind this, but presume it is a policy to keep at least one cliff as a place for individuals to explore, as though they were the first to come to it. However, in reality the regular frequenters of the Gunks, who climb 5.10 + , all seem to know about it, so it becomes accessible to out of state, or out of country visitors who meet them, but remains unknown to those who do not.

On our running circuits we had spied the cliffs a few times, the large-looking white walls tantalizingly protruding out of the trees. The route we were particularly interested in was Persistence, a steep overhanging crack with a boulder problem start, that continued to give over 100 ft of climbing and was graded 5.11. The first time we went out to the cliff Chris Plant, another British visitor, was with us. The three of us thrashed through the woods

wondering about the reliability of the directions we had been given. The trees and vegetation were thick, making it difficult to orientate oneself. The thought did begin to cross our minds that we were going around in circles when we saw the rock. Unfortunately it was the wrong section of the cliff, after more thrashing about amidst the vegetation and fallen leaves that were starting to cover the ground, we came to a large boulder about the size of Almscliff crag. Quickly we scrambled to the top of this, and there was the route, a perfect-looking line, consisting of a steep crack, with a dogleg at the bottom, going right to left. This had to be the route, the Gunks has so few cracks there was unlikely to be another one, we hadn't been told of, besides which the first fifteen feet were covered in chalk. The first major problem was to start the route safely. Between the boulder we were standing on and the first holds on the face was a five ft gap with a 25 ft drop below, and nowhere within reach to place a runner. We took turns to lean over against the wall, It was very apparent that the first few moves were going to be hard. Leaning also changed our perspective on the angle; looking face on the wall was deceptive, as it appeared to look quite vertical. However, when viewed from the side or from directly underneath it was obvious that the whole thing overhung considerably. When acquiring information about the climb we had been good rock research students, so were aware of this problem and familiar with the tactics most climbers had utilized to overcome it. Already we had acquired a stick about four ft long whilst coming through the woods, and generous supplies of tape filled our pockets. Below the route, on top of the boulder, were sticks strewn around with telltale pieces of tape still stuck to their ends. The trick was to tape a stopper, a number six, on to the end of the stick with a crab attached. It was important to have the whole ensemble only lightly taped together as once the extension had been used to place the nut the stick needed to be removed. Remembering to place the rope in the crab, a last minute detail we almost overlooked, the nut was securely placed.

That nut took a lot of falls during the day; we took it in turns to try to make sense of the holds available, and how best our bodies could be positioned to maximize their use. Chris tried direct tactics and brute strength; Rosie resorted to an offset layback almost remaining in balance and got higher, I copied the layback style which although elaborate in its combinations, did look the most promising. Eventually we did get up the first 30 feet, but it had been very much a combined effort, with falls every time we placed a nut. Exhausted fingers finally won the day. We managed to get round to the top and abseil down to retrieve the gear. It was quite a shock to see just how far out from the rock the ropes did end up; they were a good 15 ft out from the face, and it took several assisted swings to get in to retrieve the gear. The route would have to wait for another day.

Another day came this time with just Rosie and me. We did get a lot higher, but still both of us had to work on it to gain our high point. It was obvious that the repeated attempts were making it easier. We were remembering the sequence of moves at the start and repetition was making them flow with less energy drain. It turned out that once the first 20 ft were over it was no longer technical, but by that time the continuing steepness got to the forearms, causing them to pump up solid. There was supposed to be a rest in the triangular niche about 60 ft up, where apparently it was possible to get a knee lock then take both hands off. That day we did get up to the niche, but the next day we had plenty of bruises to testify to our fruitless attempts to get the knee lock, and neither of us had managed to take even one hand off, never mind two.

Finally we returned again, to spend yet another day at Lost City. This day really would be the last one as September was ending and it would soon be time for me to return home.

Rosie got first try, and the first moves went easily. By this time we both had them wired and Rosie made them look deceptively easy. Puffing with exertion Rosie pulled into the niche, twisting her bent leg into a multitude of positions as she tried to get the knee lock. Meanwhile her fingers were uncurling as her arms screamed out their desire for relief; they got it — plop! Rosie dangled in space about four ft below her high spot. Frustrated she demanded to be lowered to the ground. Then started a 40 minute timed rest before her next attempt. 'OK, time's up'. The ropes were pulled down and Rosie tied on, a look of determination and growing concentration on her face. 'This time, this time, do it, do it', repeated in my head like a mantra. Rosie did it! My turn? Everything went well. I pulled into the niche with arms that did not have any more pulling in them and tried for the lock off. My knee locked in position. It hurt like hell but I could take off both hands and shake out, regain a little respite and recover some strength. Only about 30 seconds were needed before I was able to continue and make the top. What a route! After the amazing amount of effort we had put into doing it, being at the top made it all seem worthwhile.

September was over, reflecting on the past month, the memory of the days already stood out as magical. The climbing had been challenging, the rock first rate quality, the scenery, sights and sounds had been beautiful, and finally Rosie Andrews had been an inspirational climbing partner for me. New England as it turned out had been a wonderful choice for rockclimbing.

Jill Lawrence's first rock climb was a severe at Almscliff called Bird's Nest Crack in 1973, and she has remained active in climbing ever since. A partnership with Peter Livesey saw a tremendous rise in her ability, but it was not until she climbed extensively with other women that she found the support and competition that gave her the impetus to meet the challenge of leading. She continues to use climbing as a vehicle for learning about herself.

# October: Beyond the Equinox

## JIM PERRIN

It is the eighth month, the harvest month, except that it is now the tenth, whatever it may have been to the ancient Romans. But count the days, count the lunar cycles as we will, we cannot allay loss of the green hours, or even divert the trickle of time. This is the red month, the year brittle with age and ready for the fire. The tendon snags in its sheath, the bone once broken nags its pain; but the days are so few now that we have to stumble on. The equinox is past: beyond the year's Rubicon, light gives way to the night.

You should start climbing in the spring of the year and the life — give the impulse time to establish itself before the fingers chill and winter comes. Also, because you are set thus in the cycle your senses feel no dissonance between activity and age, attune more directly therefore to that which we should notice in the environments amongst which we move: the jackdaw chicks which hissed at our hand in that April crack; the hyacinth fragrance of bluebells beneath those boulders in May; or purple-veined Lloydia around us in all its delicate rarity as we lay on that Devil's Kitchen ledge the next day — all are chiming with our green age. Memories accumulate, to enrich in the long perspective the landscapes they inhabit. Come October, comes their synthesis, and the time to gather, revisit, relive.

Let the magic be encountered early. Do you know that painting by Turner, *Norham Castle at Sunrise*? It is all yellows, mauves, ochres and almost gentian-blue shadows, utterly saturated with colour yet delicate withal and unformed, the shapes unresolved, shimmering, optimistic. There is perhaps a valley, a castle, a cow, but as yet we cannot quite tell for behind the picture's gentian heart the sun's presence is veiled, not stated. It puts me in mind always of the October days in my first season's climbing. Do you remember what it was like to be awakened by daylight on your first outdoor mornings? You are in the Grand Hotel, say, as the carved name above Robin Hood's Balcony Cave at Stanage calls it. Your companions (having had a skinful of beer in The Scotsman's Pack last night which you, as a thirteen-year-old, could not afford and were not allowed) are still snoring. You slither, in your sleeping bag across the sandy floor, out of the entrance, over to the lip of the ledge and look out beyond. The cold air of morning on your bare shoulders causes you to shiver a little and shrink down in your cocoon. In front of you, from the pupa and chrysalis of the night, are being enacted the birth pangs of the butterfly day. There is a seawash and a swirl of white mist in the valley floor. It is all in motion, vaporous tongues licking at elephant peaks which laze on a white savannah: Win Hill, Lose Hill, Bleaklow, stretched out, with the sun not yet risen behind you so the colours are muted — but they will come, the bracken will crackle aflame amongst spectrums of heather, the mist will boil and distil, suggestion will resolve into form. It will all happen before your eyes on this autumn morning of your youth with much of your life before you and the whole day in which, perhaps, to climb.

Gritstone is the rock for autumn, the rowan fronds bright-berried across its grey-green walls, the leaves gathering to rot down in the dank undercliff, the fairy toadstools in the woods beneath. Its scale is all so appropriate. The day is less expansive now, the intimacy of the crags keys in to the season as if the months' passage had shape-softened them into their blunt roundness of character. Every year an Indian summer, or so it seemed in youth. It is not the great memories necessarily which remain. They have become too token, too oppressively of their stage of life, too often relived. It is the small glimpses come at by chance which retain their capacity for surprise. On a London train, during dull discussion at a committee, or sitting on your child's bed waiting to read him a story when he comes from cleaning his teeth, suddenly you're transported to *that* climb, *that* October day so very long gone. It is here now! There is no continuity. It is a single frame, a still from the life-film, a scene you had always left on the cutting-room floor in the editing of your own story. Wait now — let me focus. There is a boy, slim and dark-haired, the rock and his clothes both drab against the autumn leaves. He is looking up, holding the rope, shouting encouragement. I turn to listen, half-irritated, testily ask to be let concentrate. This is what I am concentrating on — a scoop just above knee-height in the surface of the rock, a ripple rubbed clean by the wear of feet, a rawness, pink flesh of sandgrains showing through. It glows in the afternoon sun. The rope runs down freely into his hands, no runners. He is 30 ft below and to one side. There are boulders beneath. Grains of sand, solidified, bite into the soles of my boots. I can feel them intensely, not in their individuality but in their effect. His voice comes up again, intrudes into my enjoyment of the feel of my body, its springy relaxedness on this sloping foothold, its caress of the round edge which I must somehow use to pivot around, to impel me upwards to that hold three feet out of reach above. The mind is at work, grappling with aesthetic conviction, calculating moment and force, and all of it instinctively done. My right fingertips, wrist cocked, squeeze the edge. I palm the rock with my left hand, leaning that way, curve out my knee and lift the rim of my right boot in total enjoyment of the precise, easy movement as it places itself just so in the scoop. And then — it is happening — the electric impulse from foot to hand to hip, and their suave hoist, reciprocity and interlock. Ah! I have made of those moves an elegance! I have done them well! There is happiness, smiles, relaxation. It will sustain me tomorrow in school as I stumble through the conjugation of irregular Latin verbs which I ought at this moment to be learning. It all fades. It is all gone. I am back on my son's bed with *The Magic Paintbrush* in my hand again and the first time I ever did Sunset Slab on Froggatt returns to the brain cell which holds it, to delight again, perhaps at some future time, or to die in darkness.

The companionship, the friends you have made, figure large in these memories. Good days in good company have their own rich warmth of flavour to impart. Roll the years forward more than two decades from that scene on Froggatt, and an October day in 1982 flickers on to the screen. Stanage again, but this time with Jill Lawrence. We drive down to it through all the furls and rolls of purple moorland by Langsett and Ladybower. If I had been taken out of time for those twenty years and were suddenly returned to the scene, the contrast would astonish. The crowds swarm, cars are parked on either side of the road in either direction for half a mile and more. The climbers themselves are so different. All the fawns and ragged greys, and tattered jumpers, the rusting krabs, the furry grey stiffness of nylon ropes and slings, have given way to bright multiplicity of colour and a purposeful adornment of equipmental intricacies. Yet the gaiety of outward show, the harlequin pants and jingle of rock and friend, is balanced by a seriousness of demeanour. These climbers are intent on acquisition, on attainment of objectives. Things will not just happen, they will be made to happen. It is not a world in which the friends with whom I grew up could easily have belonged. I try to imagine characters like Arthur Nirk and Pie-can and Brian Sullivan dressed up like this and behaving like this, and laugh aloud at how they would have relished the former, rejected and ruined the composure of the latter. But our old anarchic world of *outside* is subsumed now into convention and formality.

Still, we have arrived and parked at Stanage and if we look along the crag, there are great gaps in the crowds. It is only by the collectable routes that the people mill and gather. We walk up along the broadening track with the hillsides around not vibrant as they are, say, in spring, in evening sunlight after rain, but pulsing with a soft resonance of light. It is easy at times to understand those old theories of the objects of vision transmitting not reflected but their own light to the eye. It is like the miracle of sitting by a fire of coal or wood on winter evenings and feeling in its heat and flame the release of energies born of ancient sunlight.

We arrived at the crag. Geraldine Taylor had just come down after a session working on The Dangler and that induced more positive thoughts. If ever a route had offered gender-stereotyping, even down to the matter of its name, it was The Dangler — the big, butch, macho crack which real men with real muscles forced their way up, the whole scenario replete with images of sexual energy and violation. Yet I remember Barry Webb in a drunken play swinging unroped across its roof on his way back from the pub. I remember the

**Right and far right** *Jill Lawrence leading Tower Face Direct, Stanage Edge* (Jim Perrin).

last time I did it, a year or two ago, cocksure and keyed in to memory bank like a jaded lover going through the motions. But at the lip, my fingers on the edge, the programme went blank. I pulled up, people watching, the last runner too far back, arms weakening, unable to reach the top crack, panic and impotence hovering, the memory-message insistently pleading the move's straightforwardness and ease and the body crying out that it was not so, this ridiculous conflict continuing until the logical mind stepped in: 'Look, old chap, you just throw your right elbow over and get in an arm lock.' Ah, so you do! Panic subsides, tension dissipates, laughter supervenes. 'Just thought I'd do a few pull-ups for exercise, Pete,' I call down, and afterwards expiate this arrogance by confessing to him my forgetfulness.

Jill and I talk with Geraldine. She is excited, fired by a desire, insistent, working logically on mistake and weakness, psyching up for the next attempt, at which she will get it right. It is so good to watch someone in that honest and painful process. We move along the crag, take the traditional entry into a day by soloing the Rusty Wall routes — up Rogosity, with its skip-and-cling of a 5c first move; down Green Crack; up Rusty Wall of the pinch-and-lurch, down Via Media; up Via Dexter, cautiously, and down Oblique Crack. The feel of the rock, the sense of its friction, the tuning of the body-pitch, is achieved. We move on. It is to be a day on the classics. Harding's Super-direct finish to the Cave Innominate comes first, a wild swinging one-armed jug-pull right at the top of the crag and surely one of the best fifteen-foot routes in Britain.

We pass on through the crowds and fetch up at Pedlar's Slab, snort with disgust at the chipped hold at its base and work through its three-route repertoire — the slab, the arete, the rib, soloing again, building up an ease and support between us that relaxes into the climbing and enables us both to move better and more rhythmically. It is the desire that the other should enjoy the routes that is coming out, and not that so-often-dreadful-in-its-effect

an effortless, rhythmical quality quite different to the thrusting economy of the best male climbers. Their characteristic is a lightness, a fluidity of movement centring around the pivot of the hips, an exquisite and almost formalized balance like that of Indian dance.

The crowds have drifted away as we work back — though work is the wrong word for this activity — along the crag. The light's going as we descend, and there are different points of the compass to which we must head. She goes north, my way's west. There is a spontaneous embrace by the cars at the recognition of how it was, a brief, warm, laughing, — one of those moments of contact which make endurable the deserts of solitude — and all's then given over into October memories, harvested and stored away on the long drive west.

West is the real October country. There is the low-angled light slanting into the hills and against the cliffs. There is the way the richness of texture in rocks, the veins and foldings, the crystals and the ribs and the stippled lichens soak in the soft brilliance of the sun. There are the hillside woods like old tapestry or brocade, which seem to tell of stories set there. Wales — the text of its landscape is more resonant than that of any other country. All the stories and histories have that autumn twilight quality, diffused and haunting and lingering down the sterile times of winter coming — for an industry, for a people, for a culture. They are so old, as old as the year in October. They rustle their suggestions amongst the quiet places of the hills, the soft clatter of their names like leaf-fall in a forest. In that oak-tree roosted the eagle from whose flesh the maggots fell. This split rock here was cleft by the flung spear. But it was so long ago. The barracks of the quarrymen who came after that time, they are occupied now by the elder and the ash. Where the kettle hissed after the day's work, the leaf falls; where the fire flamed, the rowan flames. That wall blew down in the equinoctial gales, but who knows how long ago? It is gone, the memory, just as this year is going to join it, just as our years have added something before they rot, or are lost, or used up from the long store.

October, you are crowded with ghosts. Here, walking by my side over the road from Deiniolen with the morning sun in our faces, is John Brazinton. I am not even sure of the year — the autumn of 1969, perhaps, or 1970? We

game where the other must be outdone. On Pedlar's Rib — my own route and one of which I'm inordinately proud — I step up blind-footed and ask if my boot's on the hold before moving on. She guides it there. At her turn I stand beneath, confident and aware of what she can do and remind her of the hold not obvious from where she is. It is the brief gestures, the respectful minimalism of assistance, the arm slipped round a waist and then away again, in friendship and support, which state the harmony, and thrill and thank. The day goes on: The Unconquerables, Goliath's Groove, Wall End Slab Direct, Tower Face Direct. There is a cool, gold wind blowing across the crag and a rhythm of chatter and silence between us. On Tower Face I watch her face on those creaking flakes which make the climb far harder that its given grade of HVS 5a and marvel at the honesty of emotion portrayed there: alertness, apprehension, the awareness of vulnerability. It is all so different to the non-expression of rock technocracy. The bodily movements too have trek on foot from Deiniolen to Llech Ddu, the wild ponies winter-coated now and watchful across the Afon Llafar, the grass bleached tawny summerlong by the sun and rain, the path squelchy with moisture. It is a return visit. Once before this same year I have come this way — to climb The Groove with Brian Fuller, that strange, sardonic, yet likeable member of the Rock and Ice and Bradford Lads generation whose nickname was Fred the Ted. We had arrived beneath the great soar of rock up which The Groove cleaves its way, sat down to talk and gear up, and heard a whistling in the air above us. A sheep, fallen from a ledge 400 ft up, landed 20 ft away, spattering us with blood and intestine. We joked about it and wiped ourselves clean, we were disturbed by another whistling in the air, and the same happened again, at almost the identical place. We felt nauseated. Minutes passed. We roped up, studied the first groove. A shadow hung in the air above us, whooshed past and exploded by its two former companions. We felt hunted, and crept away to a quiet VS round the corner.

But this time, with John the mood is lighter. At 19 or 20 he is my apprentice and I, at 22 or 23, am supposed to be the young star and we want to do the route as near free as can be. Mo and Cam (neither of them ever known by anything other than these names), who did the first ascent four or five years beforehand, had given perhaps the only completely honest first ascent description written for a post-war route in Wales, mentioning every point of attachment used, whether for aid or gardening. Either through malice or uninformed gossip, thereafter the climb had been looked on as overaided, with four or five aid-points in 400 ft.

It is odd how fragmented your memories become over long periods of time. Only three sections of the route come back to me. There is a wet, loose, dripping bulge somewhere near the beginning — perhaps on the second pitch — where I had to layback on a downward

*Jill Lawrence soloing Wall End Slab Direct, Stanage Edge* (Jim Perrin).

spike which moved out towards me as if daring me to see what would happen if I pulled harder. There is a traverse left across a steep wall, with hard, blind moves into a shallow groove where a sidepull came off in my hand and I nearly swung off with it, and turned to swear at John for no better reason than that he was the only thing around who would take any notice. Finally, there is a stance in slings in the groove itself from which The Groove gets its name, and the near-disappointment of just pulling from hold to hold in an easy ecstasy of strength. I remember very little, then, about the route, nothing about getting back down to the foot of the crag, only vaguely recall the peaceful trudge out along Cwm Llafar towards the evening sun and the descent in darkness into Bethesda. But it is as clear as yesterday to me, the pleasure of going into the Douglas Arms and finding Keith Carr there in a corner of the front room.

Keith was a member of the Wallasey Mountaineering Club, which was one of the liveliest and most anarchic organizations ever to have graced the society of Welsh climbing. It had its heyday in the late 'fifties and early 'sixties, and was based at a club hut which was a converted barn set on a hillock right in the middle of Nant Gwynant, beneath Clogwyn y Wenallt. The club had close associations with Ogwen Cottage before that place became the staid outdoor centre of a local education authority. Its members were people like Mo Anthoine, Davey Jones, Ginger Cain, Terry Vasey, all of whom were climbing at the very top standards of the time, but it wasn't as a climbing ginger-group that the Wallasey was well-known. It was the originator of the tradition of the wild party which reached its climax in the Al Harris Bacchanals of 15 or 20 years later. The barn in the Gwynant was the perfect site — no fear of intrusion, objection or the giving of offence. The beer would be imported by the barrel, there would be none of the strobe-and-disco suppressions of the demonic imagination on the crutches of

*Dick Griffiths bouldering at Criccieth West Beach* (Jim Perrin).

which today's party-goers lean. Instead there were the evil geniuses, the out-drinking, out-phasing and out-grossing gamesmen (and women) and performers, all thrashing around in pursuit of the fiercest squeal of shock or outrage the evening could produce.

It was over these times that Keith Carr, John Brazinton and myself squawked and joked this October evening in The Douglas, and continued late into the night back at his house in Mynydd Llandegai before John and myself walked back to Deiniolen over the moor in the moonlight, with the sea glinting down in Caernarfon Bay and the light of Llanddwyn Island flashing out to us. It may sound degenerate, but then it was fun, as naive and feckless as children's play. But the play's gone, the summer's over, the nights are drawing in.

John and Keith, with whom I reminisced those many years ago, are both dead: John killed by stonefall in the Chamonix Aiguilles the season after we did our route together, having volunteered typically to go back up to the foot of a route to collect his and his partner's sack, and Keith, in his forties, of cancer or some other such gratuitous disease. All along your path you lose the friends you make and only your memory keeps their names alive: John, with whom I enjoyed a single day's climbing of a quality I've not often known; Keith, in whose warmth and wit I've basked and revelled in many times in the pubs and convivialities of the climbing world. The months, the years draw on. The leaves fall.

Let me go to the sea to rid myself of this despondent mood! One seaside weekend of

*Tony Shaw bouldering at Craig Isallt* (Jim Perrin).

*Bouldering at The Roaches, Staffordshire* (Jim Perrin).

*Jill Lawrence leading the Left Unconquerable, Stanage Edge* (Jim Perrin).

October springs to mind. It is 1972. I'm living in London at Ken Wilson's flat but he, arch-enemy and sometime friend that he is and has always been, is not coming on this trip. We are going to Pembroke, which is unfashionable — so much so that Colin Mortlock, myself and a very few others are the only ones to have climbed down there. 'We' are John Kingston, Rob Ford and myself. On the Friday we set off in John's Sunbeam Rapier down the M4 to Cardiff and we bear on down through Morriston and Pontardawe, Carmarthen and St Clear's, rattling on all the while in one of those wonderful London weekend protracted arguments which passes away the long driving hours and covers every topic from politics and the Stock Exchange to sexual anthropology and the invertebrate life of Hemel Hempstead before bringing us after midnight to the deserted and derelict cottages (National Trust holiday lets now) at Stackpole Quay, where we creep upstairs, spread out our sleeping bags on the dusty floor, and rap out our concluding comments before sleep rules all further discussion out of order.

The next morning we breakfast on cream cakes in Pembroke and walk across the untrodden, clean-washed beach of Barafundle to Mowing Word. All those miles of coast along to Stack Rocks from St Govan's, where new routes were done in their hundreds in later years, we ignore. We are not here to pioneer and don't feel like the mental strain involved in that. All we want to do is disport a little on known rock in the late-season sun. We solo down Square Chimney, always a good little test piece to see how the nerves will cope with the day's climbing. On the wave-platform beneath we skip across the razor-edged scallopings and walk to the tip of the promontory. The sea's in a lovely green calm, with waving fronds of weed clearly visible deep down in the water. I point out the routes. We traverse round beneath the south-west face, the sharp rock nicking and grazing at our hands, and gather beneath Cormorant Flake, with the water idly trickling into the little coral pools. I've been thinking that a combination of the first pitch of Heart of Darkness and the top pitch of New Morning would be perfect, so persuade John, who's enjoying the rock and the scenery, to lead off. I psyche him up for it: 'Once you're round that arete, John, it's a hundred feet across an overhanging wall into a bottomless corner, and

then forty feet out to a hanging stance!' What I'm omitting to tell him is that huge holds, good jams, ease the strain of the hugely impressive situation. He launches out, disappears round the corner, and is soon chortling with glee. Rob follows, and at John's insistence, to reverse the joke takes all the runners out. The ropes swing across a void. I reach the corner and gulp down my anxiety: 'You bastards!' I shout across. 'V Diff!' John retorts. I know it's not that, and scuttle across before my arms tire. We move on up to a higher stance and I hustle for the top pitch: 'It's all jamming, this, John — you'd better let me lead!'.

He does. I exult in it, a perfect thin crack running up an otherwise blank head wall for 70 ft, the rock a gorgeous bright orange colour from the sunlit lichen. The jamming's a joy — there's surely no more satisfying technique of climbing, nor any which is more elegant or relaxed. You stretch, place the jam, arch your back, run up your feet, jab in a toe, lock in one-handed, stretch and arch again in a smooth, unhurried flow. It is sensuality in movement. You ration runners to keep the aesthetic line of that rope running down, to conserve strength and maintain the thrill — one good one every 20 ft will do! Rob and John run up and rave. We slither down Square Chimney again for another route or two, then give best to the incoming tide and repair to the pub. The next day we go to Mother Carey's Kitchen (which sounds like a local name but isn't), do a few routes, recover a sling left behind a month or two before, already bleached white by the sea, and as the tide comes in again we pack up and drive vociferously back home. Weekends away! What a habit and delight they once were! But the month's ending. November looms. The clock, which goes always forwards, has gone back. Hallowe'en, All Soul's Night, Samhain, all the pagan festivals of fire and darkness concentrate in the mind.

At this time of year the memory always comes back of one particular friend who represented much of what I loved about the world of climbing, with whom I had many of my best times on rock — Al Harris. He died in a car crash on the way to a party in Chester in the late October of 1981.

Either the cars or the parties were bound to have got him in the end. There was the party of the JCB Joust, when two of those machines

*Snowdon from Moel Siabod* (Jim Perrin).

had been left in a field by his house and Harris's idea was that the perfect game would be a wrestling match between them. So the whole of Bryn Bigil resounded nightlong to the sound of heavy rock music, screeching metal and roaring diesel engines as the mechanical monsters wrestled each other to the ground. Or there were the chicken matches at what's now Dinorwig's Bus Stop Quarry, when Harris had laid in a stock of scrap cars and we took them up there, unhooked the gap in the wire netting specially cut for the purpose, and sent them screaming over one by one into the dark water, their doors taken off first so that we could jump out the more easily at the last minute — Al, Tim Lewis, Nick Estcourt — all the lovely boys whose smiles are dust, all gone before, all burnt in the fire, and the last leaves hang grimly, limp and tired on the trees. I must walk out on the hills; it is depressing me too much to think of what has been, of all the dead playboy friends of this western world.

I drive to Cwm Ystradllyn near my home, walk up to the shoulder of Moel Hebog by way of the old, hidden and deserted quarryman's village that has no name beneath Braich y Gornel. The mist circles the hill at the level of the shoulder. It is full of presences, my mind peoples it with memory, projection and desire. With shortening breath I pant upon the slope. A stonechat chips away at silence from a rock. Where the steepness begins to relent, the cloud thins and soon blue sky's above, and a cold wind chills across my face. I wipe the drop from my nose and leave its stain on the light green of my sleeve. Obdurately the body paces itself to the summit cairn, the rough brown rock around it solid, solid, solid to the touch.

Beneath me now Nant Gwynant is fading into shadow, the brilliant golds and ochres, the yellow and orange of the trees mutely retreating out of the light, the lakes lying leadenly amongst them, the knoll where Menlove's ashes were scattered standing out like a peacock's crown in a twilight garden. Behind me, the sun is setting out at the point of Lleyn. Ynys Enlli, the Isle of the Currents, of the Saints, hides its western Avalon or Eden behind the hump of a hill. I know about Saints, have known some in my time, of all shades from self-abnegation and denial to voluptuousness. Sainthood is the perfect expression of reverence for creation, and Dostoevsky's underground man will tell you, even if by default, as much about that as the theologians can. It is getting dark now. The slope steepens in the descent. Only Bryn Banog lies before me to complete the circuit, and Moel Ddu, the black hill, which I must cross before I reach home.

**Far left** *Tony Shaw bouldering at Craig Isallt* (Jim Perrin).

**Middle left** *Roger Alton on New Morning, Mowing Word, Pembroke* (Jim Perrin).

**Below left** *Jim Perrin bouldering at Craig Isallt* (Author's collection).

**Left** *Climbers on The Strait Gate, Mother Carey's Kitchen, Pembroke* (Jim Perrin).

Jim Perrin was born in Manchester and started climbing in the Peak District at the age of twelve. During the 'sixties and 'seventies he was generally regarded as one of the foremost rock climbers in Britain, putting up a great many new routes. He worked as a climbing guide and instructor before going to university to study as a mature student. He carried on to research for a PhD in seventeenth century political biography. Since then he has written prolifically on climbing and environmental topics and is an important features writer with *Climber* magazine. He is married with four children and lives in North Wales.

# November: Two Sides of the Mountain

## ELAINE BROOK

Boots crunched in the frost. Thin air rasped and burned in dry lungs. On the summits of Transerku and Ama Dablam, sun gilded the snow and haloed the peaks against a pale sky. It had yet to reach us, plodding, earthbound, up the steep rocky trail. Lhakpa was ahead, waiting. When in England he scorned exercise, yet the first few days of trekking had brought a rapid return of his inherent fitness and already he was striding ahead of the rest of us, matching the pace of the local Sherpas who had never left their mountains.

I perched on a cold but welcome rock to catch my breath, while the others arranged themselves in poses representing varying degrees of breathlessness. We were slowly emerging from the relationship of guide and clients and working our way towards becoming friends. It is a process that unfolds more quickly up in the mountains, where living is pared to its necessities and the grandeur of the surroundings combined with the physical struggle seems to bring the inner self nearer the surface. You often find your companions either become intensely irritating or else you become friends for life.

John and Francesca sat together without speaking, sharing an intuitive harmony that came from so many years together. Silvered hair was the only indication that they were well into their sixties; healthy living and every weekend out tramping the fells had kept them more agile than most people half their age. Their son and his wife had spent the last seven years compiling the definitive *Birds of Nepal** and Francesca could spot a bird where the rest of us could see only tree.

Ann was scanning the shadows of the gnarled forest for signs of her husband. In her mid-thirties, she worked as a nurse in a busy hospital, and at the last minute had almost been deemed too indispensable to be spared for a four-week trek in Nepal. Her expression showed she had found what she was looking for, as a crackling of twigs and a crashing in the undergrowth heralded the rapid approach of someone clearly oblivious of gravity or personal safety. Seconds later, Yann Lovelock burst into the sunlight, his usually pale, gaunt features animated and flushed with elation.

'You can see the whole next range of mountains from the ridge up there...'

He folded his tall, angular frame on to a boulder, continuing his account between gasps for breath. His energy and curiosity seemed insatiable; he would probably know every inch of the Khumbu before Ann managed to shepherd him back on to the plane home. He spent much of his time writing poetry, in between earning his living as a prison chaplain. A devout Buddhist, he had come to the Himalaya to learn more about the origins of his faith, as well, it seemed, as visiting every ridge and minor peak in the range.

It was mid-afternoon by the time we reached Thangboche. The chill afternoon cloud had engulfed the hilltop, softening the dark smudges of the trees and glistening damp on the boulders carved with mantras.

The American trekkers who had shared our campsite in Namche were there ahead of us; they spent less time gossiping with the Sharpanis at the tea-shop by the river. They had already completed their tour of the monastery and were returning to their tents set in neat rows on the open space below the chorten, the prayer flag. I recognized the group leader, conscientiously shadowing the last straggler. 'One of your guys keeps leaping out of the forest and frightening my trekkers,' he said, a little plaintively. Yann erupted from a nearby tea-shop, brocade earflaps of his newly-acquired Tibetan hat at a rakish angle. 'Hey, come on, they've got hot chocolate in here!' The young American jumped visibly, made polite excuses, and scuttled off to join his group.

Inside, the warm, steamy atmosphere

*A Guide to the Birds of Nepal* By Carol and Tim Inskipp, 1985, Croomhelm, London smelled of cooking and coffee. Sherpas and westerners were squeezed on to the rug-covered benches around the walls, cold fingers clasped around steaming cups. The centre of the room was dominated by the bulk of a stone and clay oven. Au Tawa, the proprietor, was supervising the two teenagers who were swapping soot-encrusted pots around on the glowing fire-holes, their faces lit by the ruddy glow of the flames. He grinned across at us, and motioned one of his young cooks to pass us cups of chocolate. 'Back again, eh? How was England?' Lhakpa nodded his thanks as he took the cup. 'It's good,' he said non-committally, 'and it's good to be back, even if I do pant like a tourist walking up here.' Au Tawa laughed and ordered us a top-up. 'Uncle Monk', as he was known, not only ran the busy hotel, but was also the business

*Lhakpa Sherpa* (Elaine Brook).

administrator of the monastery. This meant a full-time work schedule, for the Reincarnate Lama of Thangboche had recently set up a Cultural Museum as an annexe to the monastery. It had made a good start with generous donations from climbers and trekkers, but was always in need of new funds.

Lhakpa slipped out for a few minutes. The Lama's personal secretary was his *tro*-brother; their fathers had exchanged vows of lifelong loyalty and friendship. Making an appointment to visit the Rinpoche would also be a good excuse to catch up on family news.

The Lama's new visiting room was light and airy, with large windows along the south side. The walls were wood-panelled for insulation – a luxury in the Khumbu these days, when all cut wood has to be carried from outside the National Park.

The Rinpoche himself sat on a cushioned bench at the head of the room. His lean, aquiline features were accentuated by his shaven head and the deep red of his woollen robe. Although there was little opulence in either his clothes or his surroundings, he possessed the dignity of one who owns nothing yet has everything he needs. He accepted our white scarves and donations to the monastery with equanimity, leaving the crumpled notes on the low table until his assistant came in with a tray of brimming teacups and cleared them away. I could see poor Francesca bracing herself to drink the butter tea out of politeness, knowing she suffered a mild allergy to milk products.

The Lama spoke clear, sophisticated Nepali, and the conversation drifted back and forth, inevitably returning to the subject of the Cultural Museum. I was interested to learn that the ideas behind its establishment went far beyond a desire to preserve precious artifacts from Sherpa homes or religious institutions. The Lama, clearly, was becoming increasingly concerned about the erosion of the values which held their culture together.

'My hope is that our many foreign visitors will be able to understand some of the deeper aspects of our culture. Perhaps the younger Sherpas, too, will see the tourists taking an interest in their background and look again at what they are leaving behind when they go running off in search of material wealth and expensive bits of Western technology.' He turned to Lhakpa. 'You are not the first Sherpa to marry a westerner and spend much of your

*Thyangboche Monastery, with Ama Dablam, Lhotse and Everest behind* (Elaine Brook).

time living abroad. But you are the first to come back and still take an interest in your religion and heritage.'

Lhakpa looked pleased and a little embarrassed. It had not occurred to him that he was any different, any more than it had occurred to him to allow living in the west to change his outlook.

The Lama continued. 'There is even land lying uncultivated in Khumbu now. The men go to Kathmandu to look for work with climbing expeditions or trekking groups. Then they get involved in business or life in the city, and they come home less and less frequently. Khumbu is becoming a community of women and old people.'

There was sadness in his eyes as well as his voice as he spoke. He was not going to say 'I told you so', but he and men like him had warned in the past that the Sherpas would bring about their own downfall if they turned away from their traditional values and codes of practice.

Outside in the fog, the muffled sound of heavy bells heralded the arrival of a line of

laden yaks hauling climbing equipment from Base Camp. The garishly-coloured tents and foam mattresses with spiky ice-axes and crampons lashed on top were in stark contrast to the winter grey and olive of the open pasture. The Sherpas who had worked as high altitude porters for the expedition were still wearing their one-piece down suits and plastic double boots, swaggering a little for the benefit of the Sherpinis carrying water up from the spring.

It was hard to believe that 30 years ago the Khumbu Sherpas would not have dreamed of climbing mountains for their living or any other reason, yet today this is the popular image most westerners have of Sherpas.

The Sherpas originally migrated from Eastern Tibet about five centuries ago, crossing the Nangpa La pass west of Cho Oyu in search of fresh pastures for their yaks. They augmented their rather poor, high-altitude subsistence farming by trading between Tibet and lowland Nepal and India, mainly using the 18,000 ft Nangpa La as a crossing point. The closing of the border by the Chinese in the 'fifties and the

**Above** *The Reincarnate Lama of Thyangboche, with Tapkhey Lama* (Elaine Brook).

**Below** *The popular western concept of a Sherpa — as an employee of a climbing expedition, carrying loads up the mountain* (Elaine Brook).

*With the recent relaxing of border restrictions, some Sherpas are once more following the steps of their forefathers and crossing the Nangpa La with their yaks to trade in Tibet* (Elaine Brook).

dwindling of their trade prospects coincided with the opening of Nepal to an increasing number of climbing expeditions. Expedition climbers had previously used Darjeeling Sherpas to carry loads on their forays into Tibet via India. It soon became clear that the Sherpas' experience of trading journeys in rugged terrain, and the toughness and stamina inherent in those who survive a life in harsh conditions, made them the ideal people to hire to carry equipment up the mountain. Soon the Khumbu Sherpas were being employed as well.

In these days when the use of bottled oxygen was considered to be the only way to succeed on the Himalayan giants, it was essential that those hired to carry it did not need to use it, or the assault would suffer from the law of diminishing returns.

Like ripples in a pond, the effects of those first expeditions had grown and spread to the whole of Khumbu. More climbers and trekkers came; people who could pay very high wages, but who had different attitudes to every aspect of life. For the Sherpas, wealth had increased; so did the number of bereaved and deserted families. Western education enabled them to compete and be more independent – and spiritual values and community spirit went into decline. The Rinpoche and other community leaders, far from trying to discourage the commerce with tourists, were hoping to channel it into a more constructive outcome.

The heavy cloud cleared in the night, and the moon glittered crystalline slivers of frost that crept across the earth. The rock and ice walls of Kangtega reared up above the tiny huddle of buildings on the ridgetop, sunk into deep shadow as the cold light silvered the snow thousands of feet above.

Yann was up at first light, exploring, taking in impressions to record in prose and poetry.

Gazing at Kangtega and Ama Dablam is sheer delight, but looking at Everest brings the strangest disorientation. I've grown up with that name, and during my boyhood it stood for inaccessibility. In my teens Englishmen were still trying to climb it and dying on its slopes. Because it has been nothing but a mental image for over forty years, I cannot make myself understand now I am in its presence. If it is real, then it must be myself that is only a mental picture, lacking in solidity. This is a good dharma of course, but the moments when we actually see the truth of our lack of inherent own-nature in our hearts are few and generally unpleasant.

...Fragile, preserved between the pages, if we could turn that leaf again and find our certainties return.

I wandered further up the ridge until I found a rock from which I could see the peaks surrounding the Nangpa La. I stayed there looking at the view longer than anywhere else I've known, following the line of little tracks winding along cliffs, or looking at the strange clouds. Whenever I'm in the mood, I still lie back and call up the view and feel the same mood of quiet and happy wonder. None of our porters would believe this; among them I have the reputation of 'hopping about worse than a flea'.

The walking during the next few days grew easier. The actual distances covered were greater, but we were adapting to the altitude, the routine and each other. Each time I return to this place, I find it has changed subtly – not just with the seasons, or the inexorable march of time, or even commercialism, but in my own relationship with its different aspects. There will always remain something of mystery, something to be discovered. This time it is as if I have become a catalyst for the experience of others, leaving me to explore the inner harmonies of this kind of sharing. It was my friend Julie Donnelly who taught me that it is not necessary to be the first, or the best, or the strongest, if you have inner peace and can share your heart with others. She became the first blind woman to reach the 18,000 ft summit of Kala Patthar near Everest, yet insisted that the attention and recognition this brought her meant far less than the experiences we had shared during that climb. For me, that expedition had opened doors of perception, where hitherto familiar places would seem new and strange because I had learned to see them with a different perspective.

The trail skirted the rocky slopes of Khumbu Yu Lha, home of the god of Khumbu. The Bhote Kosi, 'River from Tibet' foamed and growled, unseen, far below in its gorge. Dapple-shadowed, sweet-smelling pine forest gave way to open winter heath with the flame-red spiny bushes of berberis iridescent against the deep blue space of the gorge. A raven floated below us, silvered wings a fragment of the sunlit snow on the great barrier of peaks ranged like a bastion to the south.

Above the pool of valley shadow the mountain hermitage of Lawudo basked in sunlight high above us. We turned off the main trail and followed the dusty switchbacks steeply upwards, catching only an occasional glimpse of our goal beyond the towering shoulder of the hill. It had become a kind of November pilgrimage, this slow dusty plod to one of the highest oases of retreat on earth. Each time I returned, I would unconsciously renew the commitment to return yet again.

I fell into step behind Francesca, feeling a little concerned. This would be the first time in her life she had attempted to go above an altitude of 13,000 ft — and today was her 65th birthday. I hoped her resilience would not let her down. I should not have worried. She was

*Julie Donnelly: experience of an inner dimension* (Elaine Brook).

pacing herself carefully, rationing her energy. Her diary reads:

Am I really here on this beautiful morning in the Himalayas on my 65th birthday? There are magnificent snow-covered mountains all around us, gleaming white against a deep blue sky. The little temple is further than it looks, and we stop in the sun to rest, soaking in the warmth and the clear air. Thought becomes calm, remaining in the present and aware, with love.

We climb steadily; suddenly two Impeyan pheasants, the national bird of Nepal, fly out from the slope ahead, purple and green glistening on necks and long tail feathers. We crawl around in the undergrowth for a while and see five females, but it's tiring at this altitude and the stalking has to stop. We keep a lookout for lark thrushes and roseate finches such as we saw at Thangboche.

The retreat is a cluster of small buildings perched on the steep hillside, with fluttering prayer flags all round. The meditation cave has a small window and door, and is wood-panelled inside. On the sunny terrace outside, one of the nuns is sitting on the step knitting a cream sock; she breaks off and brings rugs for us to sit on. The lama's brother and sister, both in dark red robes, invite us to share their lunch of tea and potatoes. The tiny, high-altitude potatoes are yellow and taste like chestnuts - I have even learned to cope with the hot sauce!

Two American Zen Buddhists arrive; they had heard about us in the village and walked up here to ask Elaine to translate their questions for the Lama. Tapkhey Lama from Solu is visiting here, and he answers their questions, mainly about preparation for death and the next rebirth.

Tapkhey's exuberance and cheerfulness are infectious, helping us to forget our tiredness for the return journey. He will travel with us back to Solu, where he is establishing a new monastery and school for the people of his village. Already John is planning the celebration of his 70th birthday in a couple of years' time; perhaps he will come back and help Tapkhey with the wall paintings in the new temple.

As we descended to the Dudh Kosi river, the devastation wrought by the late monsoon flood became more apparent. A glacial lake high above the Bhote Kosi had burst through its moraine, bringing a 50 ft wall of rock, mud and water crashing and searing through the narrow gorge. Farms, fields, crops, and livestock had sunk into the gaping maw, leaving giant white scars of naked rock reaching barren fingers up into the green of the hillside. Mercifully, the human toll had been low: warned by the roar of its approach, most people were able to make a desperate scramble to safety. From above, they watched their homes and land disappear forever.

Sherpas on the trail spoke in hushed voices of seeing the god of the lake rise up in anger and hurl itself in a mass of ice and water at the moraine. Its first victim was the hydroelectric scheme, ten years of foreign aid money and labour, which on completion would have brought to an end the Sherpas dependence on wood for fuel. Some felt uneasy that it would then make them dependent on foreign technology and maintenance technicians instead, but in five minutes the god of the lake made such speculation obsolete.

With the removal of the protective forest layer, such floods and erosion were becoming increasingly common in the mountain areas, where the delicately-balanced ecosystem can be so easily upset. Ironically, this was the fate warned of by the Rinpoche and other lamas as the consequence of trespassing into the snow mountains, the symbol and abode of the gods.

'If we go on the mountain, and make it dirty with foul smells, the god may become angry and eventually will leave, upsetting the balance of energies in the land.'

The god, or protector of the land, is the focus of spiritual energy for the people who live there. It is the force which keeps the elements and the land in fertile harmony. Respect for the gods, controlling greed in cutting too many trees, or carelessness in polluting streams, provided the laws of basic ecology which for generations kept the Sherpa homeland balanced, productive, and fertile. When the gods leave, 'in storm, hail, and flood,' the harmony is lost and the land becomes a desert. Looking at this ravaged wasteland of tumbled boulders and shattered trees, it is easy to identify with the respect the Sherpas hold for such power. Not for them the packaged luxury of a few weeks of sport and

*The flood on the Dudh Kosi brought devastation along the whole length of its course* (Elaine Brook).

recreation in an attractive mountain area before jetting home to a world that foolishly prides itself on keeping such powers at bay. For the Sherpa, this is the difference between life and death. They must live with the mountain and its power, its fragile precious gift of fertility and its god.

From the Western viewpoint, it does not follow that to climb on a mountain will bring destruction to the surrounding area. For the Sherpa, there is less of a distinction between an action and its associated state of mind. Changes in mental attitudes bring other actions. Commerce with climbers and trekkers involved not only religious trespass, but large scale sales of precious firewood, and the forests diminished. As Buddhists, the Sherpas avoided the taking of life, yet the same commerce results in dozens of goats, buffalo, and chickens being slaughtered in Namche for the bazaar every Saturday.

Some Westerners are beginning to acknowledge the values of the Sherpas, either out of respect for their friends or for the environment they are using for their enjoyment. I remembered a conversation with the Tyrolean climber Reinhold Messner, about a mutual friend, Ang Dorjee, who had since been killed on Everest.

'On Cho Oyu Ang Dorjee spoke a lot about this god of Cho Oyu, and he had dreams, terrible dreams, and he told us these dreams. On Kanchenjunga he asked us to stay below the summit. He climbed with us, and I had promised him we would not go to the summit, so it was clear to me we would not do it. I had respect for this religion of the Sherpas, and for Ang Dorjee as a friend. But for myself, I had this feeling that it was not necessary that we should go up these four more metres. And I hope that even now nobody has been to the summit of Kanchenjunga.'

For the Sherpas, whether they are catering for climbers and trekkers or carrying oxygen

*One of the makeshift bridges on the Dudh Kosi after the flood* (Elaine Brook).

up a mountain, there is no doubt that they are making more money than ever before. What remains to be seen is whether they can maintain their culture when so many of the underlying values have to be compromised in order to make a good wage.

Would the problem be solved if all the hotels were solar-powered, and served vegetarian meals to polite, culturally–sensitive trekkers? Or if the climbers left their staff in Base Camp and climbed the mountain themselves, as Messner did on Everest? Probably not, although it could be argued that it would be a start.

For the moment, such speculation was set aside for the more immediate problem of ensuring our little party crossed the makeshift bridges perched among the wreckage without disappearing into the churning grey waters of the Dudh Kosi. Anne's diary recorded the impression these made on her:

The flooding had swept away whole hillsides, including large parts of the trail. At first this involved small detours up and down among the rocks, but on turning a corner we were confronted with a wall of loose dirt down which rocks were still falling. We could see other people negotiating this, which was reassuring, and we hurried in the wake of the path that had been stamped along the slope, and which was filling up with sand even as we passed.

We scrambled down a steep earth cliff, then hopped among huge river boulders making for where the bridge had been. Villagers had replaced the wreckage with five springy tree trunks, one sanded in the middle. Porters were sliding cautiously along this in plastic flip-flops; a Sherpini had fallen and been drowned two days before. I crossed carefully, concentrating on Tara mantras, with Tapkhey Lama following. I admitted my cowardice and using the mantra. 'So did I!' said Tapkhey, with a huge grin.

Lhakpa's sister Khandi runs the Sherpa Lodge, the largest hotel in the village of Surkye. We declined her offer of rooms and camped in her potato field, as a family of Rais were holding a noisy *chang* party in the basement. Our porters smelled the chang and went to join in the drinking. Khandi invited us to sit round her fire and drink tea, as the sounds of the merriment below drifted up through the floorboards.

Khandi's two boys clattered round helping stoke the wood fire and scrubbing pots. Only three-year-old Maya was exempt from a share in the housework. She perched on a low stool by the fire, to be fussed over by her mother and brothers in breaks between the chores. It was not just shyness that kept the child in her safe corner; Khandi feared she was slowly going blind. One eye was already glazed and white, and there was concern as well as sadness in Khandi's attentions as she searched the other eye for signs of opaqueness. The local clinics, while adequate for everyday ailments, were not equipped for specialist treatment. Maya's father was determined that she should have the best medical attention available in Kathmandu. It was this determination which kept him away from home for months at a time during the tourist season, working for the best money available –

on climbing expeditions.

The morning trail through the forest was wet and slippery with dew, and a dawn mist wavered in soft white tentacles between the houses of the village below us. High above, the snow peak of Kwangde glistened in the first rays of sun. The superimposed images in my mind – the ethereal beauty of the goddess and the quiet tension in the house below in the village will always remain, vivid and powerful. The Lama's dream of a balanced synthesis of east and west, old and new, became all the more poignant when the situation touched friends and family. 'If only', you find yourself saying, if only we could have hospitals but not climbing accidents, new schools but no drift to the cities... and so on.

The Sherpas call the sunlit side of the mountain *nyimare* and the shadow side *rhibshang*, the two complementing each other to make the whole. The Eastern philosophy of balance – yin/yang, feminine/masculine, earth/heaven – could also be seen in terms of east and west. Who can say that the western view of a mountain as a challenge is any more or less valid than that of the Sherpa who regards it with veneration as a deity? Like sun and shadow, the two philosophies could be seen, not as opposites, but as complementary in a balanced whole.

As the sun rose towards its zenith, the shadows on the goddess Kwangde shifted and changed, alternating light and shade in a recurring cycle that had begun when the mountain first rose from the sea.

**Elaine Brook is English/Canadian. She is married to a Sherpa and lives half the year in Nepal and half in England. She did some hard rock climbing in the USA and Britain, then later undertook some Alpine ascents in remote parts of the Arctic and the Andes, as well as extended treks in the Himalayas.**

# December: Christmas in the Hills

## HAMISH BROWN

December is a month of unpredictable pitch and putt weather. We like to consider it a winter month, indeed it has the winter solstice in its hold, but in the Scottish Highlands December weather can swing from monsoon to Arctic and back in hours, never mind days. Nevertheless hill-fanatics dream of a white Christmas: December is a month for optimists.

Winter, real apple-crisp winter, has in it a lure and a challenge that will make us suffer much and wait patiently to grab the golden days of magic. Winter strips off the soft coat of summer and exposes the bare ribs of creation. It is a world pruned of the superfluous, which cheers hearts as well as limbs weary from civilization's cloying cares. Its lonely harshness is good medicine.

W.H. Murray, whose classic 1947 book *Mountaineering in Scotland* has had such an influence on generations of hillgoers (it is still in print) states in both word and deed the preference for winter deeds. 'It is in winter that the Scottish hills excel'. Of a moonlit Bidean nam Bian he wrote 'In sheer height,

silent aloofness, beauty of form, it filled me with that despairing awe that comes to all of us occasionally. Merely to have seen that beauty for a few minutes, to have felt as I felt then, seemed worth any sacrifice and hardship.' December is worth waiting for, matching solitary man to scintillating allure.

> I envy solitude
> and silence among the coloured hills
> I envy wind and stars
> and all the gossamers of life
> that man can see but cannot touch
> or rule, or legislate.
> Waves are not asked to queue,
> nor mountains wait.

The romance of the mountains that draws us to the hills is an elusive thing. It comes out of mystery, and even if never really understood, it is about us all our days. We cannot conjure it up. In C. S. Lewis's phrase, we are 'surprised by joy'. 'A day of glory given,' was the term an old keeper friend of mine used for those odd

**Right** *The Cairngorms from Airgoid Bheinn of Bein a'Ghlo* (Hamish Brown).

**Far right** *Kintail: winter in Scotland adds much to the setting* (H. M. Brown).

days which come unexpectedly, without forecasting or likelihood, and present us with splendour. I had one during the run up to Christmas past.

I had been out at weekends through November into December and had had a reasonable enough time even if there was a lack of snow to please all my skiing friends. The fieldfare and snowbunting still flew in from the north. Winter had to be somewhere. The week before Christmas the dog, Storm, and I headed off to the hills for the festive season. We crossed the Cairnwell to Deeside. Not a streak of snow was to be seen on the sorry slopes of the resort. The next few nights slowly turned the tops grey, if not white, and then it went from being *'Dreich'* to being *'Mayar Dreich'*. In Bob Scott's old bothy at Luibeg the rain and hail battered on the roof. The fire went out from lack of wood. I retreated to headphones and watched the candle shadows, while discovering the aptness of Bruckner's Fourth Symphony to the situation.

The alarm went off at six but the rattle on the roof meant it could be forgotten. Day just intensified the wet. I cycled out to my van at the Linn of Dee, with many a stag eyeing laden bike and roving dog and trotting off disdainfully into the pines. With an eye on a remote Munro the dog had not climbed I did a repacking for cycling in to another bothy base, then drove over to the valley of the Gairn. It was raining on Gairnside too so it would be warm pedalling with waterproofs on. A mile up the track I remember I'd not packed candles. Back we went. Two miles on the chain snapped and lay, adder-like, on the track. A half-hour fight (in sleet) followed before that was dealt with. The other five miles went safely but by the time we reached the bothy there was a mix of snow, wind and dusk. Our secure base was very welcome.

We lit a fire after supper and as I had a good book and music I enjoyed the evening and tried not to notice the clattering and banging on the roof or the white that covered the window and crept in under the door. The hunting winds were loose. The blizzard would probably go on all night, so I did not even set the alarm. If the storm stopped, the silence would wake me. I slept until long after daybreak.

It was only then that the silence came: the muffled, breathy, silence of deep snow. I could hear an occasional grouse complaint, a dipper chased its own voice up the river, but these were the sounds of belongings, mere accessories to the fancy. When I opened the door a thin wall of blown snow was left in the gap. All the walls and the north-west side of every tree was plastered white. There had not been all that much snow but the gale had enjoyed doing things with what it had. The world sparkled with light.

The sun could not reach the bothy because

**Right** *Cairngorms. The sneck and Beinn a 'Bhuird from Ben Avon's summit barn* (H. M. Brown).

**Far right** *Five Sisters of Kintail* (H. M. Brown).

of the shape of the hill across the river but the big hills up the valley and Brown Cow Hill behind the bothy were ice-cream white, melting deliciously in the sun. We let out a yell of glee and dived back inside to hurry up the mundane necessity of breakfast. I had gone down to the river to brush my teeth when I spotted a Land Rover creeping up. It proved to be two keepers out after hinds (two corpses in the back dripped their blood on to the snow all day) and here they swopped over to a tracked 'Snowcat' for the upper-valley reaches.

They had to cull 100 hinds each year to keep the beasts healthy, they explained, a task often made difficult by the vast scale of the landscape and the weather conditions. 'Aye, it's nae a bad day a'ta',' had been their greeting, in resonant Aberdeenshire voices. I hoped their tracks would make cycling easier the next day. It had been very wet coming in and all water would be ice now.

We set off up the burn from the bothy but soon had to climb out of its depths as the snow had piled in deeply. A bit further on we could see the whole south-east flank of Brown Cow Hill and worked out a route to bypass all the deepest drifts. It was heather moorland, loud with grouse and full of charging hares. Poor Storm didn't know where to look! At one time there were five hares rushing off in different directions. I'm sure they run the risk of jet lag when they suddenly stop and sit up, working their radar-scanning ears.

A burn came down a gash direct from the dome of hill and in the hollow where it met the moorland a score of deer were clustered. As it looked like deep snow this was puzzling. We were more than a mile away but were seen at once and the deer closed up and filed off round the hill, leaving a dark line on its white sweep. The hard work of teasing out a route to avoid drifts, bogs and drains kept eyes and mind busy so we were on the plateau edge of this huge sprawl of hill before really looking around. Wow! The whole world was white!

Ben Avon alone loomed higher than we were and its odd warts or tors (here called 'barns') stood up like sword blades in the sun. Lochnagar lay in the eye of the sun but Mount Keen and Morven were Indentikit paps breasting the Dee to the east. The poet Bryon knew these hills and wrote affectionately about them, describing a temperature inversion on Morven and making several mentions of Lochnagar in his poems. While the dog sniffed around I had a good look at the Lecht Road, that Cockbridge to Tomintoul route so familiar from radio announcements proclaiming it being blocked from snow. It wound a black snaky line up through the white so was probably all right for my escape tomorrow.

We went off in search of the cairn of Brown Cow Hill. It proved to be a wee scab of stones on the bare back of the beast. Some would decry this part of the world as 'just heather bumps', 'pudding hills', or, sins of sins for any hills, 'dull'. Such designation usually is a comment on the commentator, not the landscape. No hill is dull nor, as we saw here, does it have to be above the plimsol line of

3,000 ft to top the pops — or is it pop the tops? I sat on top for half-an-hour, just mesmerized by impressions: the magical sliding scale of the hills, from the wild white panorama itself to the tiny patterns of stars clinging to blades of grass. To be able to sit for that time was also unusual. The freezing temperature felt quite comfortable as there was no wind and the sun shone golden from over Lochnagar.

We circled round to descend by that direct gully we had seen coming up. Gravels and soil had washed down and on this fan grass grew rather than heather — which was why the deer had been there. The drifts in places had completely levelled over the 10 ft deep gash and in others had scooped out extraordinary shapes: snow sculptures — undeservedly impermanent for much worse things are shoved (all too permanently) in art galleries. We stumbled back over the heather moors, the powder snow glittering in sunbursts as we kicked it up while, behind, we left a dark line of track. There were more grouse than I had seen in years and scores of white hares, some which sat until we were only yards away.

We went up Ben Avon for Storm's Munro the next day and that huge sprawl of mountain was no better (and no worse) than douce Brown Cow Hill, just different. Frozen ruts ensured an exciting escape on the bike, with several tumbles into the drifts, but the road over the Lecht was clear and that night we slept in the dormobile on the Dirrie More, Deargs to the north, Fannichs to the south.

Over the next ten days we picked off the last of the dog's Munros north of the Great Glen then, from Nancy's hostel, made an in-out trip to Culra Bothy for the hills facing Ben Alder above the Bealach Dubh. The dog anointed his last Munro on Beinn Eibhinn, which translates as 'the beautiful hill'. Two dogs have now dragged me round these irrational listings. Please, nobody give me a dog again!

Deep winter is a time when bothies come into their own. Heavy boots and crampons, heavier sleeping bags, heavier all-sorts-of-things makes for a hefty pack just when the winter hobbles of short hours of daylight and harder conditions underfoot make life harder. It is a good time not to be camping but, having said that, some of my most memorable camp sites have been December pitches in forgotten corries or cosy forests. One such Christmas Day found a small party of us on a site between Beinn Liath Mor and Sgorr nan Lochain Uaine with our view looking out across Glen Torridon to the eagle-miles of Liathach in all its winter glory. That was an excursion from Gerry's hostel at Achnashellach where, for 13 years in a row in assorted company I have spent Christmas Day. Christmas dinners, memorable events, did not always occur on Christmas Day. Achnashellach runs to the Highland idea of time with no word so desperately urgent as *mañana*

It is interesting to see how meteorological conditions work out on Christmas Day and from my record book I can give the score back to 1961. Christmas Day that year was perhaps the coldest camp I have ever known. A friend and I were under canvas up Glenfinnan and our eggs froze solid inside the tent. (We just *felt* we had frozen, having inadequate sleeping bags.) In 1962 a school gang bivouacking inside the wooden hut of Strathcarron Halt due to a mix up of travel information. We had to climb up and fill the lamp on the signal with paraffin to operate it and so stop a train the next day. 1963 also saw us camping in Glen Carron, recovering from a long search for a missing walker. There had been several feet of snow in the glen, but on Christmas Eve a violent thaw cleaned it and probably saved the life of the benighted hiker.

Beinn Eighe was the good peak of 1964 but I missed 1965 because of frantic packing for three months away in the High Atlas. A big fall of snow halted all transport at Blair Atholl in 1966 so we just camped there and went over the Ben-y-ghlo peaks on Christmas Day, an amazing world of white again. An otter tobogganing on the flank of Carn Liath was an unforgettable sight. In 1967 we were hut-bound by a deluge in Glen Torridon. 1968 was a rare family Christmas, but 1969 saw Conival and Ben More Assynt giving a brilliant day. We sunbathed at Achmelvich that afternoon. In 1970 we were flogging out from Shenaval, but in 1971 we were plying up Lake Malawi on *Ilala*, a look-alike of *African Queen*. In 1972 came the camp looking to Liathach, the start of the years based on the cosy private hostel at Achnashellach.

The following year, 1973, produced another deluge but we made it a memorable occasion by practising river-crossing techniques in the flooded River Carron, experience we were to be glad of when facing Arctic rivers the following summer. The whole strath seemed to be flooded and the river powered down in a dirty, dark surge. Waist-deep in the river I suddenly felt my waterproof overtrousers disintegrate. The force of the water had simply burst open all the stitching of the seams. Fuar Tholl as a climb rather than a walk in 1974 was a complete contrast.

1975 was a wash out. We battled up a 1,769 ft bump above Glen Douchary as a token gesture. 1976 yielded a climb of Sgurr na Ceannaichean which was soon to be promoted Munro, an unexpected bonus that made some of the gang smug. An Ruadh Stac and Maol Cheann-dearg gave a tussle in 1977, and 1978 saw us managing only a 395 ft hill above Loch Carron's seaward end: hurricane *and* rain that day. The intriguing hill of Sgurr Dubh and its Torridon neighbour Sgorr nan Lochain Uaine restored confidence in 1979.

The 'eighties began well with a double traverse: Ceannaichean — Moruisg — Ceannaichean (1980) and a spell-binding ascent of Slioch in 1981. Two up, two down: in 1982 we festered in Gerry's (good fire, good book, good music, good company, good malt and to pot with silly hills!) and in 1983 we just went and got wet exploring the old pony track from Achnashellach up to the Coulin Pass which is now 'lost' in the surge of spruce that clothes the glen. Fionn Bheinn in 1984 was a wild but exhilarating day and 1985 began a run of Christmas Days in Fife rather than at Gerry's. So there it is: of the last 25 Christmas Days maybe half a dozen have been vile, just as many have been superb, and the rest in between. An average sort of average which would probably hold good for any day in December. September is the end of the dandelion days of summer, October sees the fires of autumn damping down, November is often grisly and unbearable, somewhere in December we are given the glory of the snows.

Though I missed Christmas Day itself one year because of preparing for Morocco I did escape afterwards in a desperate dash to try to claim my last two Munros before the January departure. As a friend put it 'It would be a shame to be killed in Morocco having left just two Munros to do!'. As time passes *accelerando* I'm aghast to realize this is now a score of years ago. It feels far more recent but I suppose such a landmark does stick in the memory while others slip into obscurity. The needed pair were Sgurr na Coireachan and Sgurr na Ciche on the edge of the Rough Bounds of Knoydart, not the most accessible area for an impecunious lad with no transport of his own. Thus it was I stepped off the train at Glenfinnan some time after midday, still a far cry to Sgurr na Ciche and a train back the following evening.

Glenfinnan was an empty glen in those days with no new lodge, road bridges or forestry plantings. I left my tent and other gear at the station and dropped down from the viaduct to the old path up to the ruin of Corryhully, walking in a fine rain, then climbing into mist on the steep pass between Sgurr Thuilm and the Streaps. Thaw-heavy snow counterbalanced any gain from a light rucksack. The pressure of the venture and the muggy, claustrophobic feel of that pass induced a real feeling of loneliness instead of the normal elation at being off alone, 'free as the road, loose as the wind'. A last Munro should be a festive social affair I decided — an 'interpersonal recreative sociality' as I once saw something described in best outdoor education gobbledegook.

Several buildings on the map offered the hope of some shelter and, for better or worse, I went to Kinlocharkaig first. Even then it was an abandoned building, insalubriously floored with sheep droppings. In a drizzly dusk in the gloom of winter it had to do. Once I'd scoffed game soup, bangers and mash, stewed apples and cream, coffee and Christmas cake it felt almost comfy — as comfy as you can be on a grisly night with all windows and the door open to the exploratory winds. I dried out a bit and wore some damp things inside my sleeping bag to dry them off overnight. Over the last hot drink I carefully checked my logistics for the next morning. I would need all of twelve hours — which meant a 4.00 am start.

Under those circumstances I hardly slept at all, being so concerned about not oversleeping. At least I set off on time. My log book described the weather as 'utterly disgusting — mist right in and rain and thaw on full blast'. Ah well, we can't have marzipan on every morning. The burns were galloping down, 'horseback-brown', the ground was sheeted with water and the snow, higher up, had the consistency of a biscuit which has fallen into a cup of coffee.

Cold was the one thing I was not going to be. The wet did its nasty habit of creeping up from feet to stockings to trousers: 'Wet below the waist-line' to misquote T. S. Eliot. My wandering torch picked up several herds of deer. When I passed they were too miserable to do more than shake great haloes of wet and hunch back into their misery. With considerable relief I found there was a bridge over the Allt Coire nan Uth. I followed this stream for a bit and then vaguely zigzagged upwards as, eventually, such a progression had to end on Sgurr nan Coireachan. The new SMC *Munros* guide calls it 'an unrelenting grind'. Daylight on top simply proved a wetter sort of grey. The snow had gone from most of the crests which was a bonus for where I had to cross snow I often went through, an

exhausting flounder every time. It was an ascent of Glen Shiel steepness with a final short snow ridge to the summit. As the descent was at a similar angle I had a pause at the Bealach nan Gall before tackling the Garbh Chiochs which could be seen bulging bare rock out of the sluggish clouds.

This is a ridge I've come to know well since but in those circumstances it was a soul-destroying place. Thank God it had a wall along its endless rocky lumps and bumps. At least that helped navigation. Now there is a certain irony, with hindsight, for Garbh Chioch Mhor has been promoted to well-deserved Munro status. At least I haven't had to make a special journey back to climb it! As *'Garbh'* means 'rough' and *'Chioch'*, is 'pap-shaped', the Gaelic name is damnably accurate. Coire nan Gall to the north is as rough as anything out–with the Black Cuillin. The fugitive prince came this way after Culloden, in the dark.

The wet rock, ambushing snow bands, rain and cloud lasted all along the dislocated ridge to the narrow col before Sgurr na Ciche: the Feadan na Ciche as it is called — the chanter of Sgurr na Ciche — which can be apt on a windy day with the wind fluting through the gap. Sgurr na Ciche is craggy but ledges led me up leftwards along the flank to reach the ridge that runs down to the head of Glen Nevis and not long afterwards a shattered trig point indicated the summit. Munro 277: no more to do. On the train home I wrote: 'Sad, as it was fun, sadder as never again would there be a new Munro (little did I know!); glad that it was the last on this day at least, glad as Ciche has rejected me several times before, glad because it is no end anyway. Most of all I want to do all the Munros in real winter conditions.'

Catching that train was epic. A quick calculation on Ciche showed I would have to average 3 mph to Glenfinnan. I ran off the mountain and at the Strathan bridge emptied everything I could from my rucker before the haul up the pass. Legs were feeling it in the end but we made the station in time to brew and repack and slip into dry clothes. The train even came on time.

The Christmas period has usually seen us moving on to Kintail on Boxing Day or soon after for my local climbing club maintains a bothy near Glenelg and it has become traditional for members to gather there to see out the year. It is not the season for pointing walls or laying floors so the atmosphere is more festive, in keeping with the season. The last month, last hour, last minute of the year will run out by a blazing log fire. Because of the long nights some residents may never actually see the bothy in daylight. If out on the hill departure tends to be pre-dawn and the return after dark. With the notorious Mam Ratagan to cross to reach the bothy there is a certain gamblers' cheerfulness. You cannot always be sure of a 'cordial snowstorm' (John Muir): too much snow and you can't travel, too little and you end with a mere icing on a brown, Christmas-pudding landscape. Cold is never the enemy: hard frost helpfully freezes the bogs and keeps boots dry, while the sky shivers its stars in brittle glitter or gives a weird touch of 'the northern dancers'. Inside you can guarantee an atmosphere which could be exported as Best British Fug.

A typical day from the bothy? We will take one in Glen Shiel, which yielded Munro Sgurr na Sgine, climbed from the east over Sgurr a' Bhac Chaolais, which is a Corbett, ie 2,500 ft in the antique measurements. I suspect the Corbett was chosen by the dog while my friend Ben is not averse to ticking off a Munro. Some day people will realize that Corbetts are every bit as rewarding as Munros and perhaps do them simultaneously rather than as a follow-up. They encourage visits to new areas and, by their definition (a 500 ft clearance), often provide views superior to many Munros. I had completed the Corbetts years before, but with the new metric maps there were seventeen new ones added to the list! This Corbett lies between the seven Munros of the Cluanie Ridge and the pair of The Saddle/Sgurr na Sgine so it has very few visitors. It is worth a conscious effort to make unconventional routes. In the vastness of the Highlands the obvious, guidebook-directed, quickest, way is, too often, the dullest and should be avoided rather than followed.

Under a coronation of stars we set off from the roadside in Glen Shiel, heading up the path to the Bealach Duibh Leac, another pass which saw Bonnie Prince Charlie slip over it, having broken through a redcoat cordon further south. It is largely due to that successful escape that we now have Ordnance Survey maps. The locals who guided the prince knew the landscape, the government forces did not, so a good case was made for producing proper maps. The benefit is ours today.

We had a warm dawn plod up to the Allt Coire Toiteil, a good way of dealing with over-indulgence in Christmas fare, so paused there to recover for a while and to admire Sgurr na

*Saileag from the east. Saddle etc beyond Glen Shierl* (H. M. Brown).

Sgine at the head of the valley, for it looked as grand as The Saddle in the sunrise effects. We donned crampons for the path was often icy or filled with hard snow. The surface promptly changed to granular snow so the crampons were not really needed. Ben's kept giving trouble so Ernst and I were on top of Sgurr a' Bhac Chaolais an hour before him. Storm, the dog, has built-in crampons and with twice the number of legs covers twice the ground.

The view along the Cluanie Ridge was made dramatic by clearing clouds which spilled over the ridge in ever-changing shapes and colours: instant Henry Moore shapes which formed and melted in minutes before disappearing completely to give a day of pristine primary colours. The Glen Shiel ridges swept along like huge breakers caught as they prepared to topple over into surf: a view sublime.

My memories are of the ridiculous. On just such a day I had enjoyed a memorable traverse of several Cluanie peaks on ski but to gain the crest had found myself fighting a cornice at the head of a corrie. Wearing skis made this a bit of a pantomime and I emerged, skis and legs first, following some contortions, mercifully unobserved. The dog could not follow and had to make a long detour by one of the corrie's ridges. He is much too polite to pass

comments. We'd had quite a few other good Christmas holiday visits to the ridges both north and south of Glen Shiel. Time and lack of ambition has not seen us tackle all the seven Munros but three, four or five is reasonable and allows a variety of ridge and corrie expeditions to be chosen going up and coming down. You could spend a lifetime exploring every nook and cranny of Glen Shiel. Perhaps 277 days on these Munros is a saner option than tackling 277 different Munros. Our view west was impressive enough.

Sgurr na Sgine is a rather secretive Munro. One has to look north, out of Knoydart, for it to take on an impressive distant view. From elsewhere it is hidden by eye-catching peaks like the Saddle or Faochag, its one-time top which has had the indignity of being reduced in height to under 3,000 ft. This is the twist of unrelenting ridge rising to a cone which combines with the ragged sprawl of the Saddle to make up the classic view down Glen Shiel. *Faochag* is whelk after its shape, *Sgine* is knife; why I'm not sure, but perhaps because its east side is cut away as if hewn by a sword. Quite a few casual plans to continue eastwards from Sgine end with the aspirant peering down the eastern cliffs in surprise. We faced this arc of cliff, which straddles the east ridge, and I must

*Beinn Sgritheal* (Hamish Brown).

admit such a view was one of my hopes of the day. It is seamed with narrow gullies, every one worth a winter climb. We went to 'have a look' which is the prelude to many an escapade on the hills.

It was sunny and warm so I removed my crampons. The others didn't and were slowed considerably. Crampons have their vital moments but they can also be a menace. (I'm sure as many people go for a slide from crampons balling-up as from not wearing crampons in the first place.) A wall ran across under the screes of the east face and the screes were large and frozen solid giving the appearance of a flight of steps up to the crags. I had been tempted by the largest gully but it looked demanding enough to yell down the other two to go round and outflank the difficulties. They were still floundering about on crampons.

After a while the snow was steep and hard, so I had to put my crampons on again and was soon front-pointing up the névé with calf-muscles complaining violently at the effort. The gully narrowed and steepened and became just too steep for the dog's natural sure-footedness. Not having rope or harness he, perforce, had to go into the rucksack. He thinks this is a good skive but the heavy, ungainly moving rucksack made for a mix of slog and panic that really set the adrenalin flowing. I ended all-a-tremble on the screes above the funnel of snow at the top of the

gully. There was no sign of the others. They had probably passed and would be waiting on top.

There was no sign of them on the summit so I had a long swig at the view and made sandwiches for us all, leaving some for Ben and Ernst on the cairn and crossing the bouldery summit to the (lower) western cairn to have a fuller view of the Saddle and Beinn Sgritheall. They did not see the sandwiches so I wonder if a later party enjoyed them — or maybe they went to the ravens or the mountain mice. After a long time Ernst appeared and an hour later Ben straggled in. They had taken their own lines and been a bit gripped I gathered. Only now did they remove their hampering campons. Black clouds, shot with red, topped the western view to the islands. Day was heading for dusk already.

We descended to the dip on the ridge to Faochag and then steeply down into Coire Toiteil, which we had looked up so many hours before. Our right skyline, dropping from Sgine's summit, is known to me as Concorde Ridge. Two figures were making their way up it. 'I hope they've got torches' Ben muttered. 'I hope they find the sandwiches' I added. Years ago, Concorde made many test flights up the west of Scotland and on one occasion I

**Above** *Ciste Dubh and the Cam-ban Glen* (H. M. Brown).

---

**Below** *Summit of Sgurr a'Bheelaich Dheig* (H. M. Brown).

was descending this narrow ridge with two boys, luckily roped-up (as it was practice for the Alps), when there was an almighty double-bang as Concorde went through the sound barrier. My heart just about stopped and the kids just let go everything before frantically clawing back again. Nerves were still trembling when I heard the gentle, but terrifying, swish of a big avalanche. No avalanche could touch us there but reflexes still worked. I died a second death. A terrified surge of 30 ptarmigan swept past. The 'avalanche' was the noise of their wings!

We managed to reach our upward tracks before it became really dark. Two other walkers caught us up and, as so often, the number of torches present or working was less than the number of people present. I pushed on ahead, following the white flag of Storm's tail, so when we all gathered at the dormobile a hot brew and a glass of *Jura* was waiting to round off the day. Pony-dodging made Glen Shiel's driving more hazardous than crossing Mam Ratagan home to the bothy.

One December there was an exceptionally deep fall of snow followed by breathlessly cold conditions which turned the west into a rare spectacle of beauty. Days like that more than made up for other days when we were pinned inside by solid rain, or at best struggled up little Torr Beag with its prehistoric fort on top, the better to see the storm and strife on Beinn Sgritheal (Sgriol) the king of the local hills and

*Five sisters from Sgurr Mhic Bharraich – Ernest and Ben* (H. M. Brown).

one of the best Munros in Scotland. That deep-freeze gave three magnificent days, and the first of these was on Sgriol.

Beinn Sgritheal has always been one of my favourite hills, back to the days when we used to stay regularly with school parties at Gavin Maxwell's home, made famous in *Ring of Bright Water*. This is one I would cheerfully climb 277 times! I have climbed with Ernst in many countries but he agreed with me that Sgriol that day was as fine an experience as any ascent anywhere. Harry joined us while the rest went for yet another Glen Shiel day — 'no walk-in' being their excuse.

The bitter cold tempted some to breakfast in bed. Water in the dixies had iced over, inside the bothy. After a first cuppa snug inside the sleeping bag there was a chaos of dressing, booting-up, eating and packing all going on at once. Boots squeaked on the snow and the frost rasped at the lining of throats and lungs. Torches were switched on and the unholy day began in the last of silent night. Speech would be a desecration. The torch light glints rainbows off the snow crystals we kick up. An owl woodwinds from the Mam, a fox barks in

the distance. There is a snort and we half hear, half see ghostly deer high-stepping off into the trees. It is an occasion remembered as sharply as the present moment.

By Torr Beag and the loch to the foot of Sgriol gives a couple of hours walking. I did it in welly boots to ensure my winter boots stayed dry. The track was frozen solid but they did save a barefoot paddle and I enjoyed watching the welly-sceptics suffer the river crossing. It snowed most of the walk-in, but once I had changed footwear and we set off upwards, the day cleared. The great depth of snow made for hard work. Captain Harry is tall and lean, the Professor and I are small and squat. With Harry in front we had to make an additional step between each of his monstrous ones. Storm actually fell nose-down into one of the footprints so his back legs and brush were left waving frantically in the air. We left quite a furrow as we teased a route up to the ridge above Coire Dubh which drains this side of Sgriol.

Coire Min with its secretive lochan looked impossibly snow-clogged. The loch was only recognizable from its pancake flatness, frozen

*Aonach Meadhoin and Sgurr an Fhilarail with Beinn a 'Bheealaich Dheirg through gap* (H. M. Brown).

and buried deep in snow. The corrie headwall being too risky (avalanche dangers) we were forced into a direct assault up the east peak of Sgriol. This bulge of slope had the advantage of being swept clear of some of the snow. An icy wind blew the snow away in a glitter of diamonds as we walked into the golden light of a newly-minted day. Bare skin would freeze but, covered, we were snug and warm. The last few hundred yards was bare ice and we teetered carefully from one exposed stone to another rather than face putting on crampons. Just taking a photograph left hands frozen, with that intense agony following as they were restored to warmth again.

The sweep of ridge from East Top to summit is well under a mile but it took us an hour: leaning on the wind and staggering about under its buffeting, an exhilarating walk. We could actually see the cornice building up along the edge and at the one narrow place where the ridge rears up to the final cone we had a flounder in a maelstrom of spindrift, fighting blind and almost unable to form steps in the bottomless powder. A plume of snow blew out into the air and everywhere

cottongrass clouds were piled up into the butterwort-coloured sky, a proud propinquity of blue and silver. It was wonderfully dramatic. The Cuillin Hills, ranged against the sun, were white to sea level.

Occasionally we have rushed off to Skye in December hoping for winter on its ridges and peaks but conditions then are seldom good or long-lasting. March and April have given me my best Skye winter climbs. The islands of Rhum and Eigg were equally white this December day and it is this western mix of seascape, skyscape and landscape that makes Sgriol one of the best of all viewpoints. Applecross, Torridon, Kintail, Knoydart, the Small Isles, Skye — these form the rim of Sgriol's view — the hub of the world on such a day of glory given.

We decided to descend the other arm of Coire Min and had just set off when we met Peter, Ann and Kay coming up the ridge. We thanked them for their track and floundered down. I have never seen the west so white. Even the giants of Torridon had been mellowed into creamy smoothness by the depth of snow. Once beyond all the crags we sat and slid down into the corrie, riding on top of the small avalanches we created. I swopped back to wellies and a brisk walk saw us home in time to rush over to the forest to lay in a stock of firewood. We had a gargantuan meal and were passing the port when Donald and, later, Charles arrived, the former from London, the latter from Sheffield, both in a race to complete their Munros before the other. Who says competition doesn't enter into such things? As a close friend of both I occupied a neutral corner.

Sgurr Mhic Bharraich, the bothy's nearby Corbett, gave us a walk which was just as splendid for Beinn Sgirtheall was part of the view rather than underboot, and the next day too invoked superlatives. Such an extravagance of days of December magic come perhaps only once in a lifetime, but the memories last for the rest of our days. In case you come under the impression that all December days are as good I will end with a day of equally memorable, but opposite conditions when Ernst and I (on a later gathering) left the bothy to motor south to a Hogmanay Meet at Dalmally.

A storm had snorted and growled all night and by dawn torrential rain had been pelting down for some hours. The bothy is reached by crossing a burn and this, just too wide to leap anywhere, was charging down as a dark spate, quite unfordable. To cross, we had first to walk away upstream and then down the other bank where every normally negligible side stream set a problem. The usually ten-minute walk to the car took two hours. The forest road out was a quagmire and trees had come down in places. Glen Shiel was spectacular, the summits under a pall of cloud, but the steep flanks were pouring down hundreds of torrents where normally none showed. The lower miles of the glen were flooded. The Telford Bridge was filled to the keystone of the arch. In the Great Glen the road along Loch Lochy had collapsed under the battering of waves and big bands of rubble had been dumped on to it off the hillside. Rannoch Moor was a wet-weather alternative for Dante's *Inferno* and Glen Orchy's river was a spectacle of naked power that was frightening even to look at.

I can recall several days as bad as that, one when Dave and I were at Gerry's and were out in the brunt of it (at valley level) seeing Strathcarron flooding, the road and rail routes being closed by erosion or debris avalanching off the hills. The day Ernst and I motored south, Donald and his wife were trying to escape from a bothy in Knoydart. Tempted by a rope left across the Allt Coire na Ciche Donald tried to ford its flood but was swept away, his body ending up in the sea waters of Loch Nevis a mile below. Our beautiful hills can be places of awesome and hateful ferocity.

When W. H. Murray mentioned Liathach as a winter traverse a local declared of that hill, 'She is majestic, but she is not to be tampered with'. But tamper we must for the beauty and the challenge can be irresistible. Christmas is a richly appropriate time to be in the hills for to us they are a place of peace and nativity, to console, cheer and enrich us, bestowing in the main joyful memories which will last through to the December of our years on earth.

Hamish Brown is one of Scotland's best-known writers and lecturers and, though he has explored and photographed world-wide, Scotland is both home and a very special place. Books like *Travels* and *Hamish's Mountain Walk* have been exclusively about Scotland, others like *The Great Walking Adventure* and *Hamish's Groats End Walk* have ranged from Britain to Alps, Atlas, Andes and the Himalayas. Hamish has also written short stories, and a book of poems *Time Gentlemen* and edited the anthologies *Speak To The Hills* and *Poems Of The Scottish Hills*. He has contributed to many books; in this one writing enthusiastically about winter in the Scottish hills, conveying boths its seriousness and the wonder and exhileration of Christmas in the wilds.